P9-APD-766

God's Pace

God's Pace

Stress and Psalm 23

James G. T. Fairfield

Herald
Press

HERALD PRESS
Scottdale, Pennsylvania
Waterloo, Ontario

Library of Congress Cataloging-in-Publication Data
Fairfield, James G. T., 1926-
    God's pace : stress and Psalm 23 / James G. T. Fairfield
    p. cm.
    ISBN 0-8361-9153-6 (alk. paper)
    1. Bible. O.T. Psalms XXIII—Meditations. 2. Stress
        (Psychology)—Religious aspects—Christianity—Meditations.
    I. Title.

    BS1450 23rd .F35 2001
    242'.5—dc21   00-068986

The paper used in this publication is recycled and meets the minimum
requirements of American National Standard for Information Sciences—
Permanence of Paper for Printed Library materials, ANSI Z39.48-1984.

Scripture is used by permission, with all rights reserved, and unless other-
wise noted, is from the *New Revised Standard Version Bible*, copyright 1989
by the Division of Christian Education of the National Council of the
Churches of Christ in the USA. NIV, from *The Holy Bible, New
International Version*, copyright ®, copyright © 1973, 1978, 1984 by
International Bible Society, Zondervan Publishing House. *New American
Bible*, copyright © 1970 Confraternity of Christian Doctrine, Inc.,
Washington, D.C.

No part of this publication may be reproduced, stored in a retrieval system,
or transmitted in any form or by any means, electronic, mechanical, photo-
copying, recording, or otherwise, without the prior permission of the pub-
lisher or a license permitting restricted copying. Such licenses are issued on
behalf of Herald Press by Copyright Clearance Center, Inc., 222 Rosewood
Drive, Danvers, MA 01923; phone 978-750-8400; fax 978-750-4470;
www.copyright.com.

GOD'S PACE
Copyright © 2001 by Herald Press, Scottdale, Pa. 15683
    Published simultaneously in Canada by Herald Press,
    Waterloo, Ont. N2L 6H7. All rights reserved
Library of Congress Catalog Card Number: 00-068986
International Standard Book Number: 0-8361-9153-6
Printed in the United States of America
Book and cover design by Jim Butti

10 09 08 07 06 05 04 03 02 01 10 9 8 7 6 5 4 3 2 1

To order or request information, please call 1-800-759-4447 (individuals);
1-800-245-7894 (trade). Website: www.mph.org

Dedication

*Norma and I have twelve grandchildren, some in high school,
some in graduate studies, and three in the college class of 2001.
In preparation for this book we asked each one this question,
"What do you look for in the years ahead? What are your hopes
and fears?" Excerpts of their responses introduce the chapters.
This book is dedicated to these young persons and their cohorts
around the world, our future.*

Contents

Preface

I believe that how we perceive reality is the controlling element in how we react to what happens to us from day to day. In 1977 when I was recovering from major surgery for cancer, someone told me that stress was a factor in the onset of the disease. Since I was the sixth of eight siblings to have some form of cancer, I began to read about the effects of stress in our lives. A year later, with a grant from Mennonite Mutual Aid, I began a four-year study of the literature of stress as a part of a master's program at Eastern Mennonite Seminary.

I began then to wonder what faith could do to the way we handled the stresses of life. Not all stress is malignant. We need the positive dynamic of stress to get us out of bed in the morning and give us the drive to do what needs to be done. The malignant kind of stress comes from the dissonance we feel when we are in a situation we cannot control. For most of us there are times when nothing works out the way we think it should; on the job, at school, in our relationships.

In Psalm 23 God is compared to a caretaker of sheep. Animals like sheep live in flocks and herds, with simple orders of dominance. But nothing about human civilization is ever simple, and the pecking orders become as tangled as egos and power and custom will allow. The result? Stress—often more than the body can handle. Different stresses pile up like silt in a river delta, damming the flow of the river's life. The effects start their work on us in infancy, and grow with the years. According to some specialists in stress research, virtually every ailment we suffer is influenced in some way by our response to the pressures we meet.

Some of the most stressed-out people are pastors and religious leaders. Why should persons of faith experience unhealthy levels of stress? What can a person of faith do to overcome the ravages of apprehension and anxiety? This is not a how-to book with recipes for stress reduction, there are hundreds of those available in bookstores and public libraries. Instead *God's Pace* explores the reality of God and his purposes in a pressure-packed world, a world in which we can enjoy the profound peace of a life of faith, a peace to sustain us as we discover who we are, and why.

There are so many persons who provided insights and stirred ideas into shape for this book that I could not begin to name them all, but I am indeed grateful for their counsel. My wife, Norma, and I sat in on one session of a stress-reducing self-help group for cancer patients in Asheville, North Carolina. In their offices in Cincinnati, some of the scientists with the National Institute on Occupational Safety and Health spoke to me of the effects of stress in the workplace. I talked with psychiatric workers at a clinic in Kansas and counselors, chaplains, and stress research professionals in Texas, on the West Coast, and in Florida.

So many people stimulated our growth in understanding of the grace of God that it becomes impossible to thank them individually. Yet in this project I must thank our children and their spouses, particularly Jim for his encouragement, John for theological insights, Debby and her writing skills, Sam for reaction to my views on reality, and Cathy with her down-to-earth thinking.

Finally, profound thanks to my editor, Dave Garber and his liason, Dave Hostetler, and Sarah Kehrberg for their caring craftsmanship and wisdom.

How to Use This Book

• *God's Pace* is for the personal enrichment of the private reader as well as for persons who want to study the text together in small groups or Bible classes.

• To enhance your study, biblical references are provided in the Study Guide at the back of the book.

• For the group leader or class teacher, the Study Guide provides questions you may adapt to stimulate discussion. The references point to biblical sources and background material.

In my fifteen years of living, I have found that
wisdom is earned, not given. Life is painful,
and what you do with that pain can become
wisdom. Society teaches you much about life
and petty things that go along with it,
but if you're not paying attention,
or choose to stay ignorant,
you can totally miss out on God.

—Seth

It is not what happens to you but the way
you take it that really counts.

—Hans Selye

• ONE •

The Lord
Is My Shepherd

My wristwatch always slowed down around 4:00 a.m. From then on, no matter how often I looked, it dragged its heels toward 7:30 a.m. and the end of our 13-hour shift. I never did like deep-night work; regardless of what my mind said, all my body wanted to do was sleep.

Body: "Go ahead, lie down. Give me a break."
Mind: "You're a liar. You'll stay there."
Body: "So don't lie down. Just close your eyes a little."
Mind: "Then I'll wake up under the machine."
Body: "But I can't do this much longer and you know it."
Mind: "Yes, you can. You've got to, so shut up and stay awake!"

Four of us were running two 70-foot spinning mules, two men on each 12-hour-plus-overlap shift. An earlier fire had destroyed half our spinning capacity, and until two more used machines could be brought in from New England and reassembled on the plant floor in Manitoba, Canada, we were expected to deliver.

Later, when all four machines were running, we dropped

back to nine-hour shifts and five-day weeks. But for almost seven months in 1947, we worked 13 hours for 13 days straight, then broke over the second Sunday to change shifts.

A spinning mule is too much like its hybrid namesake: stubborn, dangerous, and mean-spirited the older it gets. Our machines were old, well worn, and ill-tempered.

I was the shift mechanic and supposed to keep the monsters running, adjusting them for batch changes, and seeing to it they were cleaned and oiled.

I remember a lot of breakdowns that winter; that and the production demands we faced meant we cleaned and oiled on the run instead of when the machines were idle. It gave us a lot of opportunities to slice a finger with a cleaning hook, or worse.

The 70-foot-long carriage of each mule held over 300 high-speed spindles. As the spindles revved up, the carriage moved out on steel tracks, each spindle drawing from its supply of wool as it spun a six-foot length of yarn. After a preset number of revolutions, the spindles went into a wind-up phase and the carriage would make its return trip.

The whole cycle would take approximately 60 seconds. For about half of that time we could reach in and wipe the carriage frame, or drop the access door to clean and oil a couple of spindles, if we were quick enough.

None of us was always quick enough.

It wasn't so bad on working days. I'd get home by eight o'clock so Norma and I could spend a little time together. Life seemed almost normal—for two weeks. But then it was back to nights and trying to stay awake. I could sleep during the day—unless the phone rang. Then I'd be up and twitchy, to say the least. When I worked nights, Norma had to supply the good humor for both of us.

It was tougher for Norma than for me. I only had two machines to look after. She had an infant and a two-year-old in her care. Night feedings were her responsibility, plus looking after the boys all day long. Yet I don't remember a word of complaint from her. I don't know how she survived with integrity. But she did. I didn't.

Lack of sleep can turn "sweetheart" into a swearword, "hard worker" into a sharp-edged drone. Sooner or later even someone as healthy as a horse loses out to the flu or road rage or worse. When coffee no longer works, some turn to amphetamines and become walking time bombs.

A recent study of sleep behavior among gorillas showed they slept about 10 hours in 24. With all the problems lack of sleep causes, some scientists wonder if we aren't designed for 10 hours a night too.

But try to get it. A recent survey by *Prevention* magazine found that 30 percent of American adults, an all-time high, sleep six hours a night or less.[1] Sleep disorders constitute one of the biggest health problems in America—ahead of both AIDS and cancer—according to *In Sync* magazine, published by the Erie Insurance Group. Insomnia and other sleep disorders involve 50 million Americans and account for losses of $16 billion annually: falling asleep at the wheel, industrial accidents, and brain-fogged mistakes on the job and at home.[2] I know lack of sleep made me harder to live with.

Some experts say shift work can be made easier if the rotations are longer or if workers can be motivated with higher pay to stay on late shifts permanently.

Maybe if I'd been on nights permanently Norma and I could have worked out a more acceptable arrangement. I had time to play with the boys after I got home in the mornings as long as I could stay awake. Later in the day, I could read a story to young Jim while Norma fed the baby his supper.

But we never found out what might have been. On each two-week rotation those deep-night-hours soon became a nightmare. For the first nine hours or so I could handle my job easily. After we punched in at 6:30 p.m. the operator and I would clear the administrative details, check on batch changes, and find out about any mechanical problems. Then, barring a major breakdown, I'd try to get the machines cleaned and oiled before 3:00 a.m. then help the operator spin.

But when 4:00 a.m. came around, all I wanted to do was to lie down somewhere, anywhere, and let those mules fall apart. Integrity on the job didn't mean much when I was fighting desperately to stay awake.

By limiting the sleep we get, we create undue stress in all our systems, in body, mind, and spirit. Resistance to disease is lowered. Mental response time slows. We become more self-centered, less concerned for others.[3]

But lack of sleep isn't the only producer of unhealthy stress. Financial worries, a cheating spouse, fear for a child's safety, a nasty boss, traffic congestion, noisy neighbors, sexual harassment, racial bigotry; all these can stir up harmful levels of stress in us.

Some may think it's a new problem brought on by the pressures of modern technology, but as long as the human race has struggled with survival and relationships and injustice, stress has worked its evils among us.

One reason, perhaps the major one, is that we don't understand who we are and the reality we're living in, that greater but largely unseen reality I've come to think of as the "What Is" (essence) of God. From time to time we may get a flash of insight about God's realm and our place in it, a moment's idea that there is more to life than we're living, but the pressures of today crowd in and the flash fades, the idea disappears and we're swept up again in the struggle to survive.

The poet who wrote Psalm 23 discovered God in the midst of the incongruities and anxieties that make up life. And he discovered new things about himself that today we can put to good use. Becoming alive to a greater reality, the "What Is" of God, brings us the opportunity for a new level of experience. It calls out new uses for faith and trust, those old tools we have been given in our human construction, tools we've used to get along in our family and community life. When we begin to think there may be something more, faith gets to work in a deeper direction,[4] and our lives begin to change.

Psalm 23 has this concept behind it, that fully employed faith is a two-way street: God never does anything **for us** without doing something **to us** in our innermost being. *But only if we'll let him work at that level in us.*

We all start from somewhere, with differing backgrounds of culture and religion. I began my journey as a vaguely pagan Protestant Canadian Christian, with layers of British colonial history and American triumphalism thrown in, a heavy handicap. But God takes us where he finds us, whatever our religious traditions or cultural background, and calls us to his reality.

So how can his call help us with the stresses of living, when it introduces what appears to be a massive new stressor—learning to live within the disciplines of an unseen, hard-to-get-in-touch-with *What Is?* Don't we have enough trouble dealing with everyday reality without adding to it? For anyone steeped in the pressures and busyness of modern life, making such a change in life may seem like doubling up on stress. Furthermore if we were to undergo a life-change to some new disciplines, could we count on it being less stressful? Worth the time? Easier?

But who says life is supposed to be easy? Wanting life to be easier isn't quite in the same category as wanting life to be *better*. Is the life we're living now all we'd hoped for? Or is it just familiar? Let's be honest, many of the things we've done have turned out to be unsatisfying, wrongheaded, often dysfunctional. Sometimes downright evil. We've made accommodations to get along, to survive, to achieve what we've convinced ourselves we want to achieve, whatever the cost.

Yet unless we're too far gone to care, we've known there has to be a better way than the pressure-cooked, go-with-the-flow lifestyle we're encouraged to get into by the culture around us. Such a reality sucks us in easily, but it never sits well.

Both Maud and Stephanie know that life can be treacherous. Maud lost her husband and then nearly failed her daughter. Stephanie experienced go-with-the-flow, and it nearly broke her heart.

Maud loved Alec; he was part of her. When he died, that part died too, but not easily. Or quickly. As her doctor scribbled on her chart, Maud "went into depression," a catch all phrase for one of the most widespread of all diseases, especially among women. She hated the nights, lying alone. Maud gave up crying when she found it didn't ease the pain. She wanted to tear her heart out, stop thinking, and forget remembering. But she couldn't. So she went to work at a hospital, scrubbing bedpans instead.

Stephanie remembers. She was 15 when her father died and her mother disappeared inside herself. She and Maud had to move to an apartment near the hospital, something they could afford. A two-bedroom walk-up in a crumbling brick-and-shingle with graffiti on the walls and the scent of urine in the stairwell. It meant: a different school for Stephanie; saying good-bye to old friends; buying her clothes at the Salvation Army; watching her mother sign up for food stamps.

So later that year when Macho Man started to pay attention, Stephanie glommed onto him like putty on a window-pane.

As a sophomore in high school, Stephanie thought of her boyfriend as Macho Man. Confident. Knew who he was and what he wanted to do when he graduated. Had a green '53 Chevy pickup with mag wheels and a bench seat Stephanie got pregnant on.

She didn't mean to get pregnant in grade 10, but she did. He didn't mean to be a father, and he wasn't. By the time Stephanie had the baby, her Macho Man had another girl friend and Stephanie started calling him something else.

Stephanie grew up quickly in that terrible year of anxiety. She knew she'd been deceived, by her own inclinations mostly. She stayed on at school until she started to show and Macho Man faded. Then in March she dropped out. Stephanie might have finished grade 10, but she couldn't handle the stares and the cheap shots from some of her classmates—especially a couple of girls. To them she was stupid, careless, low rent, and maybe she wanted a career on welfare?

Stephanie didn't need to hear from them what she'd already thought many times herself. She found herself thinking differently about her life. Or, as she began to describe it, her nonlife.

She wondered if women knew more about humility than men. It seemed to her that humiliation carried a message: "You're not as smart as you thought you were. Wake up, stupid." She thought women might react to that message with either humility or rebellion. Or a little of both.

Maud knows the difference between humility and humiliation. She's now a nurse's aide at the hospital, about as low in the pecking order as you can get. Washing out bedpans is humiliation if you haven't got your humility straight. But it suits Maud. When Alec died, she took the job because it was about the only one she could find. Now she likes it. She says God gave her the work so she could see outside herself and her agony.

Both Maud and Stephanie found themselves in the meat grinder of life. When Stephanie became pregnant, Maud's anger at herself started her climb out of depression into caring for her daughter again. Stephanie got her mother back. Then when Macho Man left, both women tried to focus their anger on him. But even that didn't work.

That was when Maud chalked her own bit of graffiti in the stairwell, something another nurse's aide told her when they were talking about haughty doctors and nasty nurses and irresponsible runaway boyfriends. What she wrote on the wall defined her anxiety: "Stress is created when your mind overrides the body's urge to squeeze the snot out of some fathead who desperately needs it."

Stephanie came up the stairwell as Maud finished writing. When Stephanie read it and giggled, Maud apologized. "I'll wipe that off now," she said. "But first I wanted to put my feelings out where I could see them."

Two days later Maud was invited by a nurse to a potluck supper and Bible study. She would have refused to go to anything like a Bible study the week before. But now? This nurse was one of her favorites, kind and easy to work for. And maybe she might learn something to help put her life—and Stephanie's—back together again.

She didn't know it, but Maud was beginning to look for the Shepherd. She was about to find out he had been there all her life, waiting for her, as he does for the rest of us.

The Lord is my shepherd opens the way to survive our stresses with integrity. There is a Lord Shepherd to help us; we are not alone in our struggles.

It's never easy to understand how life can become so twisted and distressed. We get into situations beyond our control and lose our sense of direction. We try to find our way out of a maze of circumstances, yet often work ourselves into even messier tangles. Now is the time to look for the Shepherd's guidance: "Which way, Lord? How do I get beyond this situation I'm in? What would you have me to do?"

Psalm 23 begins and ends with God: the one Shepherd who knows us better than we know ourselves. Fully-employed faith operates with the understanding that God cares what we think and how we live our lives. As Moses discovered long ago, God is integrity itself, I AM WHO I AM.[5] We are called to his integrity, to right living defined by honesty, forgiveness, and generosity. Furthermore, such right living begins and goes on in a humble companionship with I AM.[6]

Everywhere in every time people have tried to "see" and

understand God, to bring the invisible closer to human experience. Yet the fear of doing so has also been there, fear of the Unknowable who might make uncomfortable demands on us.

Adam and Eve hid themselves from the "presence of the Lord God," because they refused the demands of humility in their companionship with God.[7] Adam and Eve chose to act on their own. They believed the temptation that says, "I know better."

That's the human problem, we've always known better; if we think of God at all, too often we define him in our terms, shape him in our image, listen to our own wants and call them his.

But those who came after Jesus saw him as a different Adam, breaking away from the old patterns of human behavior to establish a new way, a new understanding for faith to lock on to. The first Adam was of the "earth" and of human achievement, the second Adam of "heaven" and its power to transform the human experience.[8]

Let's go a little further with this. The gospels show us Jesus, the "breakthrough man," who gives us a clearer picture of God as the presence of integrity. Jesus incites the wrath of many of the leaders in Jerusalem when he tells them they do not know the reality of God as he does. "Whoever is from God hears the words of God. The reason you do not hear them is that you are not from God."[9]

It's a challenge of their integrity. And he angers them even more with another extraordinary statement: "I tell you, whoever keeps my word will never see death."[10] In effect Jesus sets his insight, his way of perceiving reality, against their religious tradition. Is he insane as they claim?[11] Or is he attempting to jar them loose from a misunderstanding of the *What Is* of God?

They respond, "Are you greater than our father Abraham,

who died? The prophets also died. Who do you claim to be?"[12]

Everything Jesus had taught, everything he knew of God came down to this: The *What Is* of God was to be found in human life. The active output of God's presence in our lives is "love, joy, peace, patience, kindness, generosity, faithfulness, gentleness, and self-control."[13] There's no death to a life like that, it goes on forever. It is reality. It is I AM in us.

Jesus goes on to tell his accusers that Abraham foresaw his day, saw the breakthrough of Jesus and rejoiced. But the men who heard Jesus that day did not rejoice. They ridiculed him, "You are not yet fifty years old, and have you seen Abraham?"

Jesus leaps to defend the reality of God: here, in us, now. "Truly, I tell you, before Abraham was, I am."[14] He defines for us how we can live a life more rewarding and enriching than we can imagine, through the power of the I AM of God, an integrity as close as our faith.

And no matter how long we've been at the business of life, Psalm 23 outlines for us how God can and will restore us to integrity—to right living—even when we're stressed out and suffering. It opens up to us the vast resources of renewal in the reality of God.

We may be lambs, yet with I AM as our Shepherd we are on our way to becoming something more, a new creation.[15]

There's a vast sea of information and cultures
out there, and it's changing, evolving.
I fear not being able to keep it together,
to focus who I am, that I'll waste my potential.
Yet my hope gives me an intuitive feeling
that life is not futile.

—Nathaniel

What we need, what we think we need,
and what we want are all different things.

—Lauren Sill

· TWO ·

I Shall Not Want . . .

I memorized Psalm 23 when I was 11 years old. At the Little Britain United Church, about 15 miles north of Winnipeg, Manitoba, our Sunday school teacher, Mr. Pittis, decided we could use a little more wisdom than we had shown until now.

The boys of the Occasional Class weren't too reliable when it came to the Ten Commandments: too young for adultery; nothing much of our neighbors' goods worth coveting or stealing during the Great Depression; and our restless minds weren't easy to focus on loving God when we couldn't figure out who or what he was. So Mr. Pittis settled on Psalm 23 as a way of gluing something worthwhile into our heads.

Except I got hung up on "I shall not want." I shall not want what? Was there something wrong in wanting? I craved a bicycle for about four years before I got one. The way my mind worked, if I didn't tell my parents I needed a bike, I wasn't going to get one. Same as a lot of my prayers years later, when I'd tell God of my needs again and again, hoping I wouldn't wind up with something I didn't want instead.

Then one day I realized there was another idea here: I did not need to "want," because God would see to it that, if I followed him, my needs would be met, and more.[1]

Trusting God would shift the responsibility off my shoulders onto his. Not that I didn't have to work, and work hard. Rather it was *what* I did and *how* I did it, whether my activities were what he wanted me to be doing, and was I following his way in doing them.

I know now this was the most important lesson I was to learn in life: No matter what, I should follow the leading of God.[2] It's a discipline I'll have to work at every day for the rest of my life because I'm inconsistent. If I look back over the last few months, I can see where often I have missed God's cues and done things on my own in my own way.

So part of the faith process is learning to recognize God's leading through the different circumstances that arise in every stage of life.

And one of the facts of life is that, depending on how I react, many of those circumstances produce unhealthy levels of stress.

What disciplines or techniques are people using to reduce their tensions and anxieties? Everything from progressive relaxation and regular exercise to transcendental meditation and hypnotism—alone or in combination. Add time management, biofeedback, acupuncture, alpha wave control, breathing exercises, image rehearsal, dietary supplements, assertiveness training. There are times to take medications under a doctor's care—a death in the family can be particularly devastating and can often make sedatives necessary.

Stress can be difficult to manage when you're downsized out of a job, transferred to a new location in another city, sink over your head in debt, go through separation and divorce, get hassled and harassed by co-workers, or when the value of your work is questioned. "Wants" pile up under such circumstances.

Yet "I shall not want" is the focus of the psalm writer's response, a statement of how he lives his life, whatever the stresses; this is the way he understands reality. It means he will depend upon God the Lord for all his needs, and beyond needs, for the actual direction of his life. The Lord is his Shepherd, he is the sheep.

In a world full of coyotes, being a sheep doesn't have much appeal. Yet the simile is not as demeaning as it sounds: sheep are rather simple creatures, whereas the world is horribly complex and capricious. Only the dangerously foolhardy think they have their world under control. At least sheep have this going for them: they get to know their shepherd and won't follow any other.

Our wants push us to follow someone. "Not me. I am free, independent; I don't follow anyone else's lead." Then how did I learn to read? Eat with a knife and fork? Tie my shoes? Drive a car?

Of course we follow—ask fashion designers, advertising executives, politicians. They build their careers by leading us to do what they want us to do. Even when we reject their images, we're not likely to be original in our rebellious actions.

We develop a sense of who we are by what we pick up from those we admire. We start when we're infants and we never stop adapting someone else's ideas and beliefs until we cease to think and feel and make choices and live. The most important thing we do is choose whom to follow; unfortunately, we don't always pick the right models.

Friends exert more influence than they know or than we want to admit. Parents, teachers, bosses, people we admire or fear all put on the pressure. The consumer media—magazines, radio and television, movies, and now the Internet—offer us any "reality" that will make them money. In the storm of messages we receive all day every day it's ridiculously easy to ignore the unfamiliar reality of God, a reality so different from our day-to-day lives we can't recognize it. Or won't. So "down inside" we listen to the voices we want to hear.

Almost without thought we allow ourselves to be shaped by the cultures that appeal to us. These voices shape our values and habits, how we think, what we do. We firmly believe *we* are shaping who we are becoming. Instead we are being molded by a thousand other influences.

This can happen to any of us at any time, including people who say they believe God and follow him daily. Ambition can steal in and overwhelm good intentions. Reaching for relaxation and peace in alcohol is still a major drug problem everywhere. Sexual hungers out of control have always created their own disasters.

For persons caught in these addictions, or in any other undisciplined desire, *I shall not want* comes as a welcome grace-gift of the Lord Shepherd, bringing the freedom for new strengths and new behaviors, a grace-gift available to young and old, male and female alike.

There are those people who say women are more aware of their inner furniture than men: more sensitive; right brain active. In contrast, men are supposed to be less emotional, more practical, and thus less interested in an inner "voice." Men are reported to be more tough-minded, never soft-headed and fashion conscious like women. Yet women can be as brittle and hard-hearted as the most macho of men. And men are as susceptible as women to style and fashion and the other voices of cultural pressure. Me-too-ism isn't gender specific.

The question is not whether we're followers but who is leading, and what it is we really want in life.

~

Stephanie says war is a game men play with guns when they've nothing better to do. Says she works in one of their war zones, a convenience store. After Scotty was born she started working there part-time: nights and weekends. In her first three months on the job the place was held up four times, twice by the same man in a red, white, and blue striped stocking mask. The second time, he shot the night manager; she bled to death before the emergency squad got there. Stephanie held her uniform jacket against the wound, but the worst bleeding was inside. ·

This was Stephanie's first job, and the woman who hired her had been kind to her. She told her mother through her tears and fears, "You know I need the job. But I don't need this."

Stephanie cried almost nonstop for two days and has worked scared ever since. Psychiatrists now study PTSD— (post traumatic stress disorder) working with soldiers from Vietnam and Desert Storm, kids after a massacre at their school, survivors of an earthquake. The purpose is to help them deal with anxiety and anguish, and get them back on their feet again.

But nobody studied Stephanie. Like too many victims, she's living with her fears and stresses on her own, learning a little here and a little there about herself and why she feels and reacts as she does.

At least she has her mother to talk to; over the years Maud has developed a lot of understanding about life, and now she's seeing life in the new light of God's reality.

But after Stephanie's boss was killed, Maud found little she could say to help her daughter's anguish or to answer her questions. So Maud suggested Stephanie rearrange her work schedule and come with her to the next potluck and Bible study meeting. After the meal Stephanie asked the group why God lets a gunman live and her boss die. That's all they talked about for the rest of the evening.

The next day, Stephanie told Maud she got some answers, but that she'll have to think about them for awhile.

The group gave her three principles to live by:

1. Stuff happens. Don't blame God.
2. Listen and learn—God will make sense out of nonsense.
3. Trust God and go where he takes you.

A week later Stephanie told Maud, "Maybe I could learn to trust God for myself. But if I get shot, what happens to little Scotty?" Her voice choked into growled sobs. "Then I won't be here for him, will I?"

Maud nodded, more to comfort than to agree. "I want you both safe and healthy and happy. I'm trusting God for you and Scotty as well as for me. I have to, because it's all I can do. "

Security. People want a lot of different things in life. But peel away the outer bark—the dream lists we write for Santa Claus—and the basic needs that remain involve security, food, clean water, a safe place to sleep, health, happiness. All of the above for our families and friends too.

Unfortunately, often we want more than we need. Today, as always, our lives are measured by success, and success is measured by visible criteria: power and influence as well as property and achievement. *I shall not want*—if I'm rich enough.

So how do I know if what I have is not enough? That was the problem of the rich young man who came to Jesus and asked what he needed to do to get to where Jesus was.[3] He followed the commandments, gave to the poor, honored his parents. But from all he'd heard of Jesus, there was more to life than he was seeing. The reality Jesus described as the "kingdom of heaven" did not match life as the young man experienced it. God had blessed him with wealth and its responsibilities, so what more could he expect?

We have many snapshots of Jesus and his perspective on *What Is*. This unique story confronts our modern perception of wealth and responsibility in much the same way as it did originally.

For many of us, security is a retirement plan, a stock portfolio, a home that's paid for, an adequate health plan. The force of our anxiety about financial security makes it a major stressor for us, pushing against our ethical and spiritual beliefs. Hidden in the underbrush of our existence lies the questions we're not too eager to explore, questions about reality like those that troubled the rich young man.

Jesus knew something this person hadn't learned yet. Wealth doesn't make it easier to hear or to understand the quiet voice of *What Is*. God isn't pushy; possessions are.[4] Could this man truly make himself available to God's reality while he was bound to his assets? Jesus challenged the man's priorities; the only way he'd learn to trust God instead of his wealth was to unload his possessions, then he'd be free of their demands.

Like the wealthy young man, the followers of Jesus find this hard to swallow. Doesn't make much sense for us today either—our North American culture focuses on what we possess. If you have any doubts, try to find a parking spot at a mall any time between Thanksgiving and Christmas! Our dedication to owning stuff is a puzzle to many Europeans, Asians, and South Americans though they too may be catching the fever.

Yet, like Jesus, we can make a direct connection between the commitment to possessions and the disease of our spiritual existence. At one time or another most of us have felt uneasy about the demands of our possessions. At that point, like the rich young prince, we are close to the kingdom of God. We may be ready for a new understanding of reality.

Jesus warned his listeners: They could not serve two masters.[5] We can't pour all our psychic energy into the pursuit of material success and not stunt the growth of a spiritual life longing for *What Is*. Whether to pursue our own interests or the "righteousness" of God is a choice we all find difficult to make consistently.

What we want at the moment demonstrates whose voice we're following now. No wonder we stir up stress!

Trusting God means adding something critical to our approach to daily living, a way to improve our chances of making decisions with integrity.

Some decisions grow almost automatically out of experience, based on what we've learned and the skills we've developed to do our work and live our lives. Yet if we rely only on old experience we can easily miss new insights from the Shepherd's leading. Now, how can we be sure of the insights? Will they benefit others or only me? The actions I take, will they be ethical or simply expedient? Moral or amoral or immoral?

Jesus was a carpenter, following in the footsteps of his father

Joseph. Back then, carpenters crafted furniture and implements as well as houses and barns. Like all such tradesmen he'd know that a reputation is built on doing a good job quickly, cleanly, and at the right price. He'd also know there were ways in his trade to cut corners and increase profits at the expense of the customer. Happens all the time, then and now.

Jesus talked about this to the crowds who came to hear him. He knew how people struggled to survive in an insecure economy, paying arbitrary taxes to often corrupt tax collectors. He saw the worry lines on their leathery faces, including the faces of the wealthier listeners. What he told them seemed bizarre: Look at the birds of the air—the wild ones, not the domesticated ones you keep at home. Wild birds don't worry where their next meal is coming from or where they'll sleep tonight, or whether they'll die before nightfall.[6] You should be like them, he prodded. God cares for them. Don't you think he cares for you as well? Do this: *First of all, look for the reality of God, and do the right thing with your life.*[7] Do what integrity demands. Then you will be as "righteous" as the wild birds. Not because you're better than anyone else, and religiously correct, but simply because you will be working in harmony with *What Is.*

Jesus stands out in history, not for his kindly aphorisms and wise advice, but for the tough choices in living with reality he insists we have to make. At another time, he told his listeners: "Whoever comes to me and does not hate father and mother, wife and children, brothers and sisters, yes, and even life itself, cannot be my disciple."[8] How can he say this? What does Jesus ask for, sociopathic behavior or worse? Hate my wife? Children? Father and mother? Why?

This isn't as crazy-making as it sounds. Sometimes family and clan loyalties can be so demanding you find yourself overwhelmed. Who you are or who you might become is dwarfed by the egos that surround you. A husband can dominate, a wife overwhelm, a father demand, a mother coerce. Even reaching out for the grace of God can be thwarted by family styles and beliefs.

Our role, our place in the clan flows strongly from expectations of parents and kin, and can become a straitjacket. Some rebel and flee into "individuality" as a way to reach for freedom and identity. Others take up competing cultures, escape into other environments.

For most of us, what we are, or think we are, has been defined by our response to the influence of others. But taking up a credible relationship to the *What Is* of God redefines who we are within those other relationships.

No matter our family or cultural heritage, to "see" and live in God's reality calls for a change in our viewpoint, a shift in our understanding of who we are. It isn't simply a matter of doing better or improving our moral batting average on our own. The Bible talks about becoming a new creation; our old life dies and is buried in the past; we are raised into a new life[9] with access to the strength of God to live as he designed us to live. And something more happens to us. Paul described it in his letter to the group of new Christians in Corinth. Not only had they changed in themselves, they would now be able to see human nature in a different light altogether.[10] Our judgment improves and we begin to understand the human condition in contrast to the *What Is* of God.

This is the beginning of hope: In everything we do we can draw upon the grace of God's *What Is*, continually. *It doesn't mean life gets simpler*, because we take up the discipline of learning how to live in this new relationship. We can't stand there analyzing every situation or we'd never get anything done. Instead, we act, often automatically. We do what we believe is right, even if we're not sure. Unfortunately, sometimes we're wrong.

Learning to do what God wants us to do often involves making mistakes, sometimes horrendous mistakes. Yet if we are committed to God's realm, if, as Jesus put it, we strive first for the kingdom of God and his righteousness, things will work out. We'll have our priorities straight. And working like the birds of the air at what is appropriate, we'll find that God provides what we need to live with integrity, as his new creation.

In the short term, I am most interested in just
having fun. I worry about small stuff
(where my shoes are, did I feed my goat, etc.).
In the longer run, I would like to get a job in
one of two areas: (1) a missionary to a
third-world country, (2) a marine archaeologist.
The problem is that I have to pass through
my major anxiety (namely, school) to get
one of these two great prospects.

—Andrew

The shepherd opens the gate
and the sheep follow him because they know
his voice. . . . They will not follow a stranger.

—Jesus

THREE

He Makes Me Lie Down in Green Pastures

Heavy duty stress? Try a ten-day visit from your daughter and her three teenage children that stretches into four months, 20 days, and 22 hours.

Cathy's mobile home situated on her land behind our place should have been ready to move into by the third of December. Then maybe by the 10th. Surely it would be ready by the day after Christmas. She had to be moved out of her previous house by then, clean and clear.

The four of them moved in with us in time for supper on the 26th of December (just until their own place would be ready).

Yet not until the 16th of May did they have supper and sleep in their own home for the first time. Their stay with us became a kind of trial by togetherness.

Cathy and 16-year-old Natasha slept on the sofa bed in our living room, while Ben and Seth took over the little room behind it we called "the den." It was mostly taken up by a sofa, two bookcases, and a television set.

Come to think of it, Ben was 20 at the time, and was

therefore no longer a teenager. Seth, at 14, took up twice as much space as he should have; put them both in there plus a cot, a guitar, schoolbooks, a box of clothes, a pile of shoes, and you could still close the door if you had the right touch.

Except for the weekends, Ben's alarm would go off at 5:30 a.m. and our day would start. Making deliveries over a huge territory, he'd hit home again anytime from 6:00 p.m. to midnight. Cathy's new job hours ran from 10:00 a.m. to 9:00 p.m. or later. Seth practiced for his guitar lessons after school and shared the feeding of their numerous pets and animals. Tasha—vice president of Rockingham County Future Farmers of America and on the parliamentary procedure contest team—had a brutal schedule. So Norma aimed supper for six o'clock, putting some aside for latecomers.

Golden Lab Chad and Border Collie Fly inhabited the backyard and barked at the moon, owls, and stray cats at midnight. Anytime after 8:00 p.m. I was ready for bed and resented dogs that barked and telephones that rang to delay the process. I had forgotten what it was like to live with teenagers, their intensity, and their pets.

But the Lord Shepherd made me lie down and "chill out. "

We were good friends when they moved in. We are even better, more understanding friends now. Somehow they put up with our odd eating and sleeping habits and early bedtimes. And we survived their exuberant attempts to be quiet and their stealthy late-night visits together. The grace of God turned the irritations and frustrations of cramped quarters and colliding schedules into a green pasture of empathy and compassion for all of us.

We were fortunate. We knew the congestion and confusion in our house wouldn't last forever. Many grandparents shove over to accommodate a daughter and her children, knowing the arrangement could last for the rest of their lives.

As often, it is adult children making room for aging parents. Living together may be the only way for many extended families to survive. Yet if some family members make demands others can't handle, the stresses can become almost unbearable.

Stress hurts when we feel we are losing control. In a "free" country, this isn't supposed to happen, but it does. Bills come due. The landlord wants his pound of flesh. You owe money to the bank, even the car dealer's bank. The boss says he can't give you a raise until there's more productivity, and you're already working as hard and as fast as you can. Still the Lord Shepherd expects us to "lie down"?

So often I want to push on and do what I think should be done. Lie down inside? Maybe later when it's more convenient. When I have time. When the boss isn't shouting at me.

Yet now is when I need to lie down most and let God show me who I am and why I am here and what can be done with the mess I'm in. I need to be quiet inside and discover what God wants me to learn. I won't learn a thing if I lie there and twitch, eager to get up and hustle the future.

Until we try it, we'll never know how it works. To lie down in the presence of the Shepherd can be the first step toward breaking patterns that have chewed us up. It puts on the brakes, stops us from running on mindlessly at the pace of the world around us. Psalm 23 insists that, no matter what we're doing on the outside, when we lie down in the presence of

God we give ourselves a chance to hear the heartbeat of his presence. We can listen to the *What Is* of God and find out who we are, where we are, and where we are going.

One night the boy Samuel found out that God had a purpose for his life if he paid attention and followed the Shepherd's directions.

As he grew into his calling, Samuel became prophet-spokesman of the Lord to Israel during the Philistine wars, and the instrument of God in the selection of Saul and David as the first kings of Israel.[1]

For years Samuel's mother had been childless in her marriage to Elkanah. When a boy was born, Hannah named him Samuel, because he was "asked . . . of the Lord."[2] When she brought him to Eli, the high priest at Shiloh, Hannah declared, "For this child I prayed; and the Lord has granted me the petition that I made to him. Therefore I have lent him to the Lord; as long as he lives he is given to the Lord."[3]

It was a time of spiritual apathy and moral depravity in Israel. The sons of Eli used their priestly position to extort sex from women and to siphon off the best offerings of the people for their own benefit.[4] Eli was in his old age, and although he protested their behavior, he was unable to control his sons.

Since he was nearly blind, he relied on the boy Samuel to help him in his ministry.

One night, after Eli went to bed in his room, Samuel lay down to sleep in the temple, where the ark of the covenant was kept. The Lord called, "Samuel, Samuel!" Samuel got up and ran to Eli. "Here I am. You called?"[5]

Eli said, "I didn't call you. Go and lie down again." Samuel went back to his bed. The Lord called a second time,

"Samuel!" Again Samuel ran to Eli. Again Eli told him to go to bed, he had not called.

Nothing like this had ever happened to Samuel before. Although he worked in "the house of the Lord," he'd had no personal experience with God, and didn't expect to either. He had not come to see God as a Shepherd who cared for his flock; few people in Israel saw themselves as sheep in need of a Shepherd; God had become a distant and not very real "overlord" of much more familiar local tribal gods to appeal to for good health, fertile crops, and success in war.

Ineffectual as he was, Eli was a man of faith who knew I AM WHO I AM. So when Samuel came into his room a third time, Eli realized something momentous was happening, and that the Lord was calling the boy.

"Go back and lie down," Eli told Samuel. "If he calls again, you must say, 'Speak, Lord, for your servant is listening.'"

God did call him another time, and Samuel was more than ready to say, "Speak, Lord, for your servant listens." From that point on, Samuel lived in a new understanding of the reality of God.

But it wasn't easy to get Samuel to lie down and hear the call of God.

Cathy has worked with sheep since we had our first flock when she was in her early teens. Later she worked on a sheep farm, a big one by Commonwealth of Virginia standards, with over 2,600 breeding ewes and 500 rams. As any good shepherd knows, and Cathy will tell you, there is only one way to "make" a sheep lie down. You can't trip it and sit on it; a sheep will pop up again as quickly as you give it a chance. The only way to make a sheep lie down is to let it graze freely in good pasture until it's satisfied. Then it will lie down to chew its cud. It has to chew its cud; that's the only way a sheep can digest what it eats.

He makes me lie down in green pastures. . . . I'm told the original meaning has a futuristic twist to it. God expects me to lie down and chew things over so I'll be prepared for tomorrow. And the pasture he puts me in is just what I've needed. Some situations don't look like green pastures. They seem to be nothing but outcrops of rock and patches of thistle until our eyes are opened to their opportunities. Only then can we find the nourishment we need hidden away where we couldn't see it before.

I've never heard the voice of God as Samuel did, and I don't know anyone who has. But I'm convinced that God has led me to experiences again and again where I could "hear" what he wanted me to do. I was offered choices of action as surely as if he had spoken.

It is as I "ate of his pasture" that I made the right decisions. Only as I saw him at work in others and digested his way to live was I able to make choices that turned out to be the right ones. If and when I ignored his way, his integrity, I missed an opportunity to grow. Yet even in those times when I was faithless, he remained faithful,[6] calling me to his way over and over through other experiences.

That is why the Bible retains its value for me. Even though its culture is far removed from cyberspace and the Dow Jones average, it sees clearly the human condition. We may ride jets now instead of camels, but our teeth still grind with jealousy and contempt for others, our hearts still thrive on the love and encouragement of others. There isn't much difference between the people in the Bible and those on this season's soap operas. The Bible condenses the human experience both with and without God so I can get closer to the *What Is* of his reality, his kingdom.

Some experiences took longer for me to understand and

appreciate than others. My oldest brother, Lorimer, was 24 years old when I was born. In its early years our family's young textile business had a lot of mouths to feed, so with a bride in mind, Lory opened a radio shop in Selkirk, Manitoba. In the late 1920s radio hit the public imagination as nothing else had done. Even though the Great Depression began with the stock market crash of 1929, enough people had jobs to give Lory hope for his business. For the first months at least.

By the summer of 1931, most of Lory's paying clientele had bought their radios. Sales slowed to a dribble. Then he made his last deal, a used RCA table model in trade for six bronze turkeys.

He had no room to keep the beasts at his place. My parents' house, out in front of the little woolen mill, had a big fenced yard I played in with Gosh, my miscellaneous dog. This was my last summer of freedom; in September I would start to school at Lockport, about a mile's walk south along the Red River. Gosh wouldn't be allowed to come with me and I fretted about that. How would he get along without me during the day? How would I survive at school without him? Meanwhile, summer lay before us to enjoy.

Then the turkeys arrived. A couple of those birds were taller than I. All were bigger than Gosh. They roosted on the back fence at night and grazed the grass in our yard during the day. Gosh took to whining at the back door in the morning when those flightless dinosaurs closed in on him. The things pooped lavishly and indiscriminately wherever Gosh and I wanted to wrestle. Mother did not appreciate the stains on my clothes, which she'd have to soak in a pail before washing.

I was totally terrified by those turkeys; they were aggressively curious about how I might taste. Their wings, although cropped to keep them from flying, were powerful weapons that could knock me flat with one devastating swat. I thought the monsters were around all summer, but I realize now it could not have been more than a week or two.

I suspect Mother told Lory to get rid of them after the first time she raced out to find me screaming under a pile of feathers, with Gosh barking and darting at the "things" he feared as much as I did.

We ate a lot of turkey that summer. And I buried deep inside me a new experience of fear.

Fear can produce a great deal of stress in a child. Not just fear of physical harm from an overly aggressive turkey but undefined apprehensions bred of the inability to express thoughts and feelings clearly, anxieties generated by an awakening conscience, dread of misunderstandings, and the loneliness they can create.

A child hates to be misunderstood and not to be taken seriously. I grew up in a time when children were to be seen and not heard. We were to keep quiet in the presence of adults. There was safety in such inhibitions. I wasn't expected to be cute, brilliant, or precocious, but I suspect that, like other children, I tried to get an audience anyway. Maybe the idea was that out on the fringes of conversations children could learn from their elders how to handle social interpersonal interactions. But another popular prohibition introduced an eddy of social confusion: "Do as I say, not as I do." Confusion rarely eases anxiety.

Fear, and the anticipated humiliation it hides, can stay with us all our lives. We grow up denying our anxieties, burying our misapprehensions behind a "cool" facade. Sometimes it works and we convince others we are coping with life. But then there are times we cannot even convince ourselves. Then stress has a free run at us and humiliation rears its ugly head.

"*Lie down*," the Lord commands. Lie down and learn the power of his humility and the joy of his peace. Grave and dreadful circumstances may rush at you to overwhelm and demoralize you.

Lie down, don't run around bleating. Lie down and listen for the Shepherd's voice in all the noise and "busyness" and distraction. This is your chance, don't miss it. Look inside the outside experiences.

It will take all you've got to do the only thing asked of you: Be still and know that God is there and will direct your way.[7] Exercise your faith to understand: Pray in patience, listen to God in humility, look for new insights to blossom.

The people who took up with Jesus struggled with circumstances in their lives that brought heavy loads of anxiety, tension, and frustration. We think we've got it bad now with pressures of modern civilization driving us into the ground. Yet, back then, people were exposed to stressors we know little about and wouldn't want to experience.

When our oldest was nine, Norma became desperately ill with appendicitis. It's an unforgiving disease; without an emergency operation her appendix would have burst in a few more hours. Death from infection and peritonitis would have been a possibility. What if we had been living in Galilee 2000 years ago?

The people who gathered around Jesus lived precarious and stressful lives. After his death some of them remembered the strength of spirit he demonstrated, the peace of mind in the face of criticism and censure, and they looked for meaning in their memories.

They remembered he spoke often of the kingdom of heaven and how its reality gave him an understanding of human nature that surprised some and offended others.

Jesus had a profound impact on the thinking processes of his disciples. And that impact goes on and on; people of faith are still trying to understand fully what Jesus said and did.

One thing we can be sure of: Jesus was so consumed by his commitment to *What Is* that he turned his back on his trade, his family, and his position in the community. God had given him a message: *The kingdom of God is not afar off, it is near;*[8] *not for the trained elite only but for "the poor in spirit" as well,*[9] *not in the future; it is among us now.*[10]

Early Christians took a long time to sort through all their recollections about Jesus and recognize his gospel. Just imagine, if you can, what this wonderful occasion must have been like: the laughter that rang out as someone recalled the imagery of a camel squeezing through the eye of a needle, even though the needle referred to could have been just a low door for a camel. Or how tears must have flowed when someone else remembered Jesus' compassion as he stretched out his hand to heal.

Every generation since has had to discover what the gospel meant in the next circumstance they faced. *The gospel of God is always calling us to our future.* The gospel is not about history, instead the *What Is* of God calls us to prepare our lives for the next choice we must make. We live and move and have our being in these choices, with a vast menu of "heavenly" resources made available to use in choosing to live God's way.

So when the Gospel of John speaks to our anxieties and tensions, it offers resources drawn from beyond our normal understandings. As we choose to follow the Shepherd, Jesus tells us what to expect: "Peace I leave with you; my peace I give to you. I do not give to you as the world gives. Do not let your hearts be troubled, and do not let them be afraid."[11]

That's the key: God's realm goes beyond all that we see and fear. And our trust in his green pasture gives us a peace that surpasses understanding.[12] We can rest in his strength, his command of reality, his love for us, and all that we might become.

*I like farm work, I've met some neat
people out in the country.
I'd like to be somewhat successful in
whatever I do in the future, but not so much
I'd become hard to live with. For me, being
successful would be staying as happy as I
could without hurting anyone else. I want to
be able to do things for others because
that's part of being happy.*

—Ben

*Blessed are those who trust in the Lord. . . .
They shall be like a tree planted by water,
sending out its roots by the stream.*

—Jeremiah

FOUR

He Leads Me
Beside Still Waters;
He Restores
My Soul . . .

The waters of the tidal stream were still and deep when Ben lost hold of his new spin-casting rig. He was 10 when his mom and dad brought their young family up to visit us. We were fishing off the dock at Barrachois Harbor, on a lonely stretch of country road near where Norma and I were living in Nova Scotia for two years. The harbor carried a full load of lobster boats earlier in the spring, but now we had the dock to ourselves.

Ben had paid for his new light-weight rig himself, out of money he earned doing lawn work. Now it had disappeared into the still-water slack of high tide.

Norma saw the quiet anguish in his eyes and never hesitated a beat. While the rest of us commiserated with Ben and wondered what could be done next, she strode over to a row of waste containers at the end of the dock and disappeared behind them. "Don't look!" she called out.

Above our heads a car rattled over the bridge connecting the two sides of the narrow channel. I trotted to where she crouched behind the containers, peeling off her shirt and jeans. "What are you doing?" I asked with some heat.

"I'm going after his fishing pole, that's what I'm doing." The look in her eyes precluded any further discussion. "Ask Ben where it fell in," she directed as she climbed down the timbers. Norma edged around to the front of the dock, and slipped into the cold, tidal water.

As she swam toward us, Ben pointed down. Norma tried to dive but popped up like a cork.

"Water's too salty. I can't get down. But I think I saw it down there. Give me the net."

Cathy handed her the long-handled fishnet. Norma's face dripped water as she reached up to get the handle. The tide was full and the water quiet but not for long. She'd have to find the pole soon, or outflowing currents would carry it away from the dock.

Holding on to the dock timber, Norma shoved the net into the water, pushing down as far as she could reach. She gently swept the net in a circle where she thought she saw the spin-cast rig. After long minutes of effort, she muttered, "There it is." Nobody breathed as she eased the long handle up toward the surface.

"I lost it!" Her face turned up to us in frustration, lips blue with the cold. "I had it, but it slipped off again!" She switched hands on the net and shook the strain out of her arm.

"Don't bother with it, Gran," Ben's voice broke the silence. "C'mon out. You've tried. It's not worth it."

Norma took a long look at his face again, then swung the net down deeper in the still water. Another car rattled over the bridge.

Her head went under as she pushed down against the dock. Slowly, ever so slowly, she straightened, water flowing down off her hair. Her arm raised, elbow easing out of the water, she exclaimed, "Yes! Got it!" As she lifted higher, the rod appeared with the reel caught in the webbing.

Ben's face lit up in utter joy. He lay down on his stomach and reached for the rod tip.

"Thanks, Gran. Thanks a lot. I really like this outfit. Thank you!"

As she watched Ben lift pole and net to the safety of the dock, Norma's eyes sparkled in triumph.

In the Bible the writers use earthy terms about everyday matters: of mending nets and planting orchards, of wedding celebrations and funerals. Life happens to fishermen and vineyard laborers, innkeepers and warriors, men, women, and children.

For shepherds, finding water for their flocks was an everyday task much harder than finding pasture. Water became a powerful symbol of life for a shepherd culture; there are some 600 references to water, springs, and rivers in the Old and New Testaments. Not all references are pleasant. There are floods, springs that run dry, and wells grown bitter with salt.

Today we have our own water problems. Some believe fresh, clean water is becoming more important to the world than oil. "Living water" has again become a universal symbol of life.

Jesus understood the value of symbols in explaining the *What Is* of God. As he traveled through Samaria on his way home from Jerusalem, he took a break and sat by the community well near the town of Sychar. It was noon and the disciples of Jesus had gone into town to buy food while he rested. Then a woman came to draw water.[1]

Jesus asked her for a drink. She was surprised that he, a Jew, would speak to a Samaritan woman, even to ease his thirst.

Then Jesus drew her nearer the reality of God.

"If you knew what God gives and who it is that asks you for a drink, you would have asked him, and he would have given you living water."

The woman looked at Jesus and reminded him that he had no bucket. She pointed out that the well was deep, so where would this "living water" come from? There was a taunt in her voice when she said, "Surely you do not pretend to be greater than our ancestor Jacob, who gave us the well and drank from it?"

She avoided looking into the still water.

Jesus told her that everyone who drank of the well would soon be thirsty again, "but whoever drinks the water I give him will never be thirsty. The water I give will become a fountain within him, leaping up to provide eternal life."

The woman came right back at Jesus with how handy this would be. She would never have to come to draw water from the well again. But because she was hiding from reality in her own illusions, Jesus wanted her to look into the *What Is* of God. He told her to go call her husband. She replied that she had no husband. Jesus reminded her she had had five husbands and the man she was living with now was not her husband. The woman began to see herself as she really was in the mirror of reality.

Yet she tried one more time to look away.

"Sir," she responded, "I see that you are a prophet. Our ancestors worshiped on this mountain, but you people say that the place we must worship is in Jerusalem."

Then Jesus directed her mind's eye beyond the surface mirror into the depths of *What Is*.

"Look, the hour is coming, and is now here, when true worshipers will worship the Father, not through places, but in spirit and truth."

She had seen reality. She left her water jar and went into town and told the people there what had happened. "Come," she urged them, "come see this man who told me everything I've ever done! Can he be the Messiah?"

Some of us peer into the still waters and think we look pretty good. Others can't stand what they see. The image of God we see in our reflection is distorted by self-disgust and disappointment. Despair becomes a way of life, leading to feelings of hopelessness, helplessness, and uselessness.

Maud was curious about her new friend Andrea. At their potluck studies, Andrea seemed so serene and content, yet she spoke of her past as if she had been "frozen in a freezer with the light out." Maud wondered if it was like the black hole she dove into when Alec died. The two women worked at the same hospital and met for lunch when they were on the same shift. One day Maud asked her about her freezer remark.

"I didn't like myself very much back then," Andrea explained. "Never did, I guess. My parents said they loved each other, but they would argue and quarrel over the least thing. Looking back, they seem to me to have been more adversaries than friends."

Andrea's face lost its serenity temporarily as she continued: "They treated me as an adversary, too. It was the way they lived. But I was just a kid. I couldn't fight with the ease they did; it cost me too much. So I hid inside myself, but the anger was still there. So much that I became angry with myself as well."

Maud realized she had been nodding and remembering.

"I did some stupid things," Andrea went on. "I thought of different ways to kill myself, but they all seemed so messy. So I took risks instead."

Andrea reached up to her throat and pulled a chain out of her uniform. "This was the mirror that gave me a look at what I was doing to myself." She held up a small silver cross with Jesus on it.

"We were studying stained glass in art class, and the teacher showed us some prints of cathedral windows. One was the crucifixion of Jesus. She explained that before the invention of the printing press, books and Bibles weren't available to ordinary people. So murals and paintings and stained-glass windows were used to tell the story of Jesus."

Maud saw the tension had slipped from Andrea's face. She reached for her coffee as Andrea continued. "I couldn't get the picture of Jesus dying so horribly out of my mind. The teacher told us what some of the pictures were meant to convey. She said the picture of the crucifixion was to show what it cost God to save the world. Jesus' death also shows what it takes to live as we ought to live."

Maud objected, "I don't understand. What did she mean?"

"I didn't understand then either," Andrea replied. "But I couldn't stop thinking about the picture and what she said. What I'd been through with my parents didn't seem like much after all.

"Some nights I'd cry myself to sleep thinking of Jesus dying like that. For what? So I could live like I ought to live?"

She fingered the tiny figure on the chain. "That was a new beginning for me."

Andrea put her coffee cup on the tray and pulled it toward her. She looked at Maud thoughtfully. "I've got to get back to my floor. Will you be at the potluck tonight?" Maud nodded.

"Good. We'll talk some more then."

That evening Andrea brought her soup bowl to where Maud and Zedekiah were eating together. She sat next to Maud, then spoke to Zedekiah. "Maud wants to know about my crucifix."

Maud flushed. "Well, it's not exactly a piece of jewelry, is it?"

"No, it isn't," Andrea acknowledged.

"It's gruesome," Maud responded.

Zed smiled at her. "But it tells you something, doesn't it?"

Maud stared at him. "It . . . it makes me uncomfortable. To think about, I mean."

Andrea told Zed it was a reminder to her of all that wasn't right in her life, of her weakness, and God's strength. "It's been a mirror to my soul. I can look at myself in that mirror and see what I am and what God is doing to shape me in his image."

"The message it sends has been called foolishness," Zed told Maud. "At least that's what Paul said in his letter to the new Christians at Corinth. People hear about the execution of Jesus and it seems a waste, a tragedy. But Paul pointed out that its message speaks of the power and wisdom of God. Like it was for Andrea."

One look in the mirror of reality is not enough to see who we are. We need to be led by the still waters again and again, time after time after time, to remind us of what we are called to be in the image of God. Yet whatever life we are given is enough, with his grace.

One of the first glimpses I remember came in grade one, on my birthday in February. The only time any water in the Red River became still was when the top layers froze over and turned into our playground. Kids, and a lot of adults, survived bitter winters in Manitoba playing hockey. The game would start sometime Saturday morning and wind down after dark Sunday night. Some of the bigger kids cleared a huge rink with a couple snow-pushers they made out of boards, big things with two or three handles to shove with.

With 30 or so players gouging the ice with their skates the puck became hard to handle. At midday one of the big guys would reopen a hole through the ice beside the rink and sink a pail in the river water. Then he'd slosh it across the surface of the rink. After a few pails and a few minutes we'd have smooth ice again and another game would start.

During the Great Depression ingenuity overcame the lack of money. Basic need—a pair of skates, though a lot of players skidded around in moccasins or gum boots. Chunks of one mail order catalog made a lot of good shin pads, and hockey sticks came in a variety of designs, from tree branches to old brooms and a few store-bought ones, reinforced with electrician's tape.

I didn't get skates for my birthday, not even the used ones I asked for. There was a pair of real skates in the cellar that belonged to one of my big brothers. At lunch I asked mother if I could borrow them.

"Yes, you may borrow them, but they're much too big for you."

"But I could put on extra socks."

"Why don't you try them on in the kitchen?" She wasn't one to argue, she figured I'd never get enough socks on to fill up six sizes. But she hadn't counted on my determination. I don't remember how many pairs of socks it took, but I got the skates on and stood up.

"See, they fit," I told mother. "May I go now?"

I walked down the back pasture to the river, using an old hockey stick of my brother's to balance the wobble. By the time I hit the rink I was skating—if you can call it that—on the edge of the boot as much as the blade.

But this was the real thing at last. I chuffed up and down the ice, getting in the way of serious players. A big one nearly ran over me, but he stopped in time. He looked at the huge skates on my feet and shook his head.

"Nice skates," he panted. "Big enough to be a good goalie for us. Want to try?"

This was great. None of the big guys ever said much to us little guys except "Get out of the way." Now I was going to be goalie!

Standing on my ankles between the big lumps of snow that marked the goal, I began to wonder what I'd do if the puck came my way. A couple other little kids started shooting frozen horse buns at me, so I got in a little practice.

Then the action came down the ice toward me. A flurry of sticks and a wrist shot. I squirmed to get out of the way and the puck slammed against the toe of my skate and caromed up to my nose. Blood running off my chin, I crawled away to a corner of the rink to suffer alone.

I pushed away the snow, hoping to see my nose mirrored in the ice—but blood dripped on the murky reflection. All I could see was my humiliation. Sometimes that's the only thing worth seeing, for a start.

God's favor rests on those who shrug off the unreal and return to the reality of God. When the psalmist wrote *he restores my soul,* that's what he had in mind.

There is a remarkable idea here—a restored soul. Restored to what? If I am bashed out of shape by the life I'm in, what's the shape I'd like to be restored to? Most of us would not be able to map out a different soul-scape than the one we've got.

When God created human beings—with an intellect and a conscience and a will—he said, "Let us make humankind in our image, according to our likeness. . . . So God created humankind in his image, in the image of God he created them; male and female he created them."[2]

When you meet another human, this is what you are meant to see, a semblance, a resemblance of God, complete with his integrity, his mercy and forgiveness, his compassion and right judgment and more.

Maybe we only catch glimpses now and then, obscured by what we've chosen to become. Sometimes his likeness comes as a surprise.

Norma and I spent two years in Nova Scotia getting reacquainted with our beginnings, doing some writing and reading and drawing. When we were first married, we spent a summer there, but had since forgotten about Canadian winters. Winter up there does things to roads, and when spring breaks out, so do the potholes. Mud season presents unexpected risks, turning once-frozen gravel surfaces into wheel-swallowers.

We'd been in Truro on a shopping trip, long enough for the sun to thaw the surface solidity out of our lane. I turned our pickup off the road and eased it up the slope toward the barn. Maybe if I'd moved a little faster we might have made it. Then again we might have broken an axle.

About a third of the way up the lane, the front wheels sank abruptly into soft ground, all the way down to the frame. The back wheels spun vainly in greasy mud.

After a few remarks on the nature of things, I got out the jack while Norma fetched two boards to put under the front wheels. But the jack, on its own board, simply squeezed down into the mud. Norma asked if I was having fun yet. "What's fun in burying a jack?" I responded sullenly. "We may be stuck in this 'till June."

Norma unloaded the groceries while I shoveled some gravel under the back wheels.

An old car clanked to a stop out at the bottom of the lane, victim of too many years of crushed salt and washboard roads. Two men got out, villainous looking creatures with scraggly hair, greasy clothes, and missing teeth. Their old car steamed a little, settling in the middle of the roadway.

As the men walked up the lane, the older one nodded a greeting. They looked under the front end, saw where I'd put the gravel under the back drive-wheels. "Get in," the older man ordered. "Back it easy."

I put the pickup in reverse and eased on the gas. The two men grabbed the front bumper and heaved. They didn't look strong enough to lift a chair, but the two of them lifted the front end out of the pothole and pushed the truck downslope onto solid ground.

Before I could get out, the men were already walking down to the road. "Thank you," I called after them. The older man nodded. They climbed into their car and were gone.

The image of God doesn't look like much on the outside sometimes. So if we go only by appearances we may miss it.

I wonder how much my goals and my fears
separate me from my peers? Probably not too much.
I need music in my life—singing, playing,
teaching. But in talking to a lot of my friends,
I think the big dreams remain constant—seeing
the world, getting married, having children.
I have an incredible fear of being a disappointment,
I'm always afraid I won't live up to my own
standards and, for that matter, the standards
of those I love.

—Dede

Hardship and danger destroys fewer
people than indulgence.

—Helen MacInnes

FIVE

He Leads Me in Right Paths for His Name's Sake . . .

There are so many tensions, so many distractions out there, that it's hard to find a green pasture beside a quiet pool. Yet such "oases" may be found as close as the next decision we have to make.

Life is about choices, many of them ambiguous and hard to deal with, especially when we're bent out of shape by circumstances. Near where we live now, Interstate 81 is a good way to get through the Shenandoah Valley, but since it's the main route for trucks running from northeast to southwest it's a bad route for timid drivers. You have a choice: I-81 at white-knuckled speed or the old Valley Pike through a string of towns and stoplights.

Yet stress isn't just a matter of circumstances. Harmful stress, the kind that gnaws on us like a dog worrying a bone, wells up from the conflicts and tensions we experience with who *we* are down deep inside.

We should look at stress as feedback from the situation we're in, feedback to point us beyond our anxieties to the

What Is of God and his purpose for our lives. Somewhere in the confusion is a way through, a path to integrity and resolution, if we are willing to follow God's Spirit.

Peace of mind doesn't come from an absence of activity, doing nothing in a perpetual holiday from effort. Rather, the peace of God that goes beyond our ability to measure or understand, the peace that can restore our hearts and minds in the midst of turmoil and anxiety, comes from this one thing: doing what is *right* for us at any given moment. This is the "righteousness of God" the Bible makes so much of, in both the Old and New Testaments.

It is "reality walking." By faith I take steps in what I believe is the right path for me, as a participant in the kingdom of God, and trust God will show me if I've missed it. It's not like picking up a printout of daily directions; "First, hit the shower, eat breakfast, brush teeth, go to work. . . ." Reality living isn't so simple. There are no Websites to tell me what to do or how to do it. Not even the Bible can tell me what choices I must make today.

When Scott was a toddler, Stephanie felt terribly new and uncertain at faith-walking. (She didn't realize that no one ever gets good at it, only more experienced. It's always an adventure. But it always works, if we keep our eyes on *What Is.*) She listened with intense interest to the people at their "potluck Bible study nights" as she called them. She saw something different in their approach to work, to parenting, to surviving the pressures of living.

She had told Maud she didn't know how long she could work at the convenience store, particularly the night shift. "I'm really scared of the holdups. And on toward morning I get so tired! I've caught myself asleep leaning against the cash register; don't know why I didn't fall.

"But what else can I do? Until I finish my GED I'm not going to find a better job. At least I'm here for Scotty during the day."

She told the group she felt trapped by her mistakes. "Some mornings I really hate myself and my life—but then, I see you all surviving bad stuff and wonder if I can, too."

A man with a bandana tied around his head answered, "It's more than survival, Stephanie." Dino smiled, showing a gap where a canine tooth should have been. "It's like riding a bike partially blindfolded; hard enough to keep your balance, let alone finding your way home. God's grace can steady you— that's the balance part, no matter how many horns are blowing at you.

"Then out of the noise comes a quiet voice, *'Follow me.'* And you have to listen, and keep listening. Or you won't know which way to turn."

An older man spoke, "Always the bike messenger, Dino? But what about all the other voices calling you to follow?"

Dino nodded. "Lots of voices, loud ones. Lots of horns. But only one word for the right way to go."

Stephanie frowned, perplexed. Almost to herself she whispered, "How can I ever know what to do?" Louder, to the group, "But that's too hard! How will I ever get it right?"

Zedekiah's laugh broke across Stephanie's intensity. "In a way, it's impossible, Stephanie. For all of us. But God finds a way to get through all the noise and clutter to give us direction. I can't tell you how he'll reach your heart, your mind. But he will, if you're willing to follow.

"Using Dino's analogy, you and your bike may run into a few open car doors along the way. You'll pick up some bruises. But following any other voice isn't going to keep you from getting hurt."

Zed's smile was reassuring, even if his words seemed to condemn her to a life of challenges.

"Life's a struggle, Steph," Zed seemed to read her mind. "Living by faith is simply a more worthwhile enterprise, because God's in it with you, and you will know he's there. As Jesus put it, being partnered with him makes the burden light. And as you go, you learn to lean on him more and more.

"That frees you up to live right."

Stephanie has two things to concern her about her path, her way to live. One is picking the right Shepherd to follow. The other is living up to what she finds out about the Shepherd and about herself. When she looks into the still water of *What Is*, she'll see herself against what God has created her to be. And she'll begin to understand what's expected of her.

"For his name's sake" is a peculiar phrase. The psalm writer figures that the Lord will lead in a right way for a reason, but to modern ears, "his name's sake" doesn't sound like much of a reason. That is, until you consider there's nothing more important to an individual than that person's "*name*"—*a term that includes reputation, the essence of one's integrity, the impact of one's being.* We are distinct entities with an identifiable character, the sum of all the parts we are, in public and in private.

It is the same with the Lord, who would lead us. This God insisted he was not like the other gods of the nations, pale creations of human imagination.[1] Those images may have been evidence of a universal human longing for *What Is*, but they were no more than longings expressed, and far short of the real thing. It is clear from the Bible that the one true Lord

Shepherd has had a hard time getting through to us, past our imaginings. Over thousands of years he has been expressing his character to us, and what he wants our relationship to that character to be, in many ways, through many people. He's still at it.

Various prophets and leaders have suggested somewhat different understandings about the same Lord Shepherd. Yet one certainty is clear: this God calls people to *his* way of living. The right way, not the wrong. *And only in living his way can we achieve the fullness of life we were designed for.* It is a moral life, a creative one, trustworthy and resilient, a life of integrity and "light."[2]

Jesus identified himself with the "right paths" and poured his life into the way of his Father. Not only did he ask it of himself, but he expected his followers to live as powerfully involved in the right way of the Father as he was,[3] learning to hear the Father's voice in the turmoil of the world, choosing to follow him on the right path, rejecting the wrong way.

Right and wrong. Clear concepts, right? Wrong. Pick up a newspaper and somewhere in its pages there will be evidence of considerable difference of opinion. One example: Some want public schools to teach biblical morals and ethics. Others raise the questions: Whose biblical morals? Whose ethics? We can't even agree on moral and ethical standards for adults, let alone what to teach our children and young people about them. Consider the debates on capital punishment, abortion, and pornography.

We hear that one man's righteousness is another's prison. So are we to have no "name" to live up to? Can we follow any voice and name it righteous?

For Jesus it meant living up to all that had been unveiled about the character of God's kingdom in the commandments, but not in the way demanded by the law interpreters and religious leaders he faced. He believed there was something more asked of him and of his people; following the Lord Shepherd meant the difficult responsibility of heeding the *living* law, as God's presence, his spirit, leads each one of us. Not a different law for each, not a different morality, but living up to the name of God, in faith, and with the grace of God to make it possible. Also living in such a way as to participate in the kingdom of God, in his community where we live and as we know it.

It's nice to think that God handed all the commandments to Moses on slabs of stone—but that was only the traditional beginning. In the years and centuries that followed, an industry of interpretation and development arose around the Law. Prophets, scholars, and teachers brought fresh insight, adding great new understandings of the righteousness of God.

After the collapse of Israel and the exile of Judah's elite to the area around Babylon some 2,500 years ago, a resurgent interest in the Law helped the exiles find new hope. "If we pay attention to the Law of God," the thinking went, "then we may be forgiven and renewed. God is faithful. We have not been faithful. Let's see what happens if we covenant to live the righteousness of God in our lives."

The result? Much of the Old Testament as we know it came into being, in recollections and amalgamations of older material and newer additions.

Teachers and their students pooled the accumulating material. It wasn't a planned process; the priests and lawyers and scribe-rewriters didn't call a meeting to appoint editors as if they were about to produce a faith encyclopedia. The New

Testament gathered itself much like the Old Testament, in respected writings, and edited rewritings, of hundreds of pieces of literature, preserved and passed down from one generation to the next.

One of these collections, the book of Leviticus, spells out the *behavior of righteousness* in great detail. Most of the chapters begin, "The Lord said to Moses . . . and outlined how the people were to live, with hundreds of precise directions; instructions on cleanliness: what animals they could eat, and those they should not; specific rules of sexual interaction; laws for marriage and separation; matters of justice:

"You shall not defraud your neighbor; you shall not steal; and you shall not keep for yourself the wages of a laborer until morning. You shall not revile the deaf or put a stumbling block before the blind; you shall fear your God: I am the Lord."[4]

Jesus had great respect for the Law of God.[5] But he objected to the way it was used as a club by some to abuse and control others. Jesus pointed out to his listeners that the scribes and law interpreters were trained in the commandments. Therefore, Jesus said, "do whatever they teach you and follow it; but do not do as they do, for they do not practice what they teach. They tie up heavy burdens, hard to bear, and lay them on the shoulders of others; but they themselves are unwilling to lift a finger to move them."[6]

Jesus did not make many friends among the religious authorities. Like many of the prophets before him, he spoke harshly about how carefully they obeyed the rules but neglected justice, mercy, and faith. He accused them of washing their hands and bowls before eating while being full of greed and indulgence inside.[7] So it was little wonder they took every opportunity to test Jesus on how he interpreted the Law.

Jesus was suspected of unorthodox ideas at best, heretical actions at worst. How he perceived the traditions became a constant source of debate among the scribes and lawyers. One of the respected teachers of the Law challenged Jesus to see if he had a proper view of God's commandments.[8]

"Teacher," the lawyer tested Jesus, "what must I do to inherit eternal life?" Jesus turned the question back on his challenger: "What is written in the law? What do you read there?"

The man answered, "You shall love the Lord your God with all your heart, with all your soul, with all your strength, with all your mind; and your neighbor as yourself."

Jesus responded, "You have given the right answer. Do this and you will live."

But the man wanted to push the matter further. Jesus was known to eat with "sinners and prostitutes" which marked him as a lawbreaker. Surely Jesus did not include such "neighbors" in his kingdom of God? The lawyer certainly would not, and he sought to be justified.

"Who then is my neighbor?" he asked. Jesus told him the story of a man going from Jerusalem to Jericho who was attacked by robbers, beaten, stripped, and left to die. A priest came along but did not stop to help. A Levite, another religious authority, did the same. In fact, both men avoided getting too close to the victim—some writers suggest they feared that, if he was dead, they would become ritually unclean and unable to fulfill their duties to the people. Yet what if he was alive?

Then along came a heretical Samaritan, a man who would be totally unacceptable to the lawyer who questioned Jesus. This Samaritan picked up the beaten man, bound his wounds, took him to a safe inn, then paid the innkeeper to look after him until he should return.

"Which of these three," Jesus asked, "was a neighbor to the man who was robbed and beaten?"

The lawyer replied, "The one who showed him mercy."

"Go and live like that man," Jesus said.

A lot of arrogance can go into "loving" God, a lot of fervor, and self-righteous conceit. But in the kingdom of *What Is*, love for God is proven in its actions.[9] Adoration of God without compassion for others doesn't add up.

The humility involved in caring for a neighbor with the same respect you have for your own being makes the respect you have for God legitimate and real.

The scribes and law-interpreters focused their attention on Jesus' interpretation of the law, and missed his focus on the kingdom of God. As Jesus said again and again, the hidden reality of God was at hand; *What Is* was now shown to be accessible to all.

Stephanie didn't know much about the law of Moses. Like many of her contemporaries, she knew there was a list of Ten Commandments but would not be able to tell you all of what they command. Most of us can't recite more than three or four. Maybe you shall not kill. Or steal. Or commit adultery. Then our list switches to guesses: Don't drink and drive? Look out for number one? A stitch in time saves nine? Doesn't say much for our biblical awareness. In any event, it turns out there are far more than just ten commandments in the Bible.

Maybe that's part of the problem for Stephanie—and for most of us. But the disciples of Jesus made a huge discovery. Laws, rules, and ordinances are the background against which we live, but we find our way by following the same spirit of the Father that Jesus followed. Faith living doesn't diminish the background, just gives the background its reason for being.

As everyone who tries to follow the Lord Shepherd soon finds out, faith living isn't easy. But it isn't complicated either. It takes a lifetime, but it starts now. Always now, with the next experience we face.

Furthermore, the grace of God is always, always available to show the way through all possible obstacles and frustrations and confusions. Don't take anyone else's word for it. Let your own experience of faith prove whatever it is you need to know about *What Is* and the character of God.

There are only these necessary conditions you need to meet. Love/admire/respect/follow God with all your heart, soul, mind, and strength—with all that you are. And look after your neighbor's well-being as you do your own. That's as simple as it gets. And as complicated.

Maybe one more condition: never, ever judge someone else's distance from *What Is.* It takes a lifetime to be shaped into what God wants of us, and God is not finished with that other person. [10] You can disagree with someone, challenge him, argue with her, rebuke his behavior, even leave her to her own devices—but never ever assume God is not at work somehow in some way in that person's life.

As Stephanie is finding out in her own life, a walk on the path of righteousness isn't as simple as she'd hoped. Today, in our enlightened democracies, we admire morality, ethics, and prudence. Law has become vital as the means for maintaining stability in our society. We agree to uphold the law so that our neighbor will do likewise.

Such modern righteousness is even more detailed and demanding than the early directives of Leviticus. Justice doesn't come easily, or cheaply. But if we remember that God is shaping in us the character of his name, in the substance of his justice, then all the twists and turns life must take will make sense. And the frustrations will yield to his peace.

There is only life, and we deal with what we are dealt as it is dealt to us. The future is not something I fear. I am far from being apathetic about what happens to me, but I don't worry about what the next day will bring. Because our lives are so chaotic it is both impossible and a waste of energy to try to plan for events we have not yet experienced.

—Ehren

∾

Learning demands suffering because it is painful to open the mind and the heart to new truth. Pain . . . results from the need to stretch mental muscles around new ways of viewing the world.

—Luke Timothy Johnson

SIX

Even Though I Walk Through the Darkest Valley . . .

"There is no such thing as righteousness, only pious fear of the unknown; no integrity, only expedient self-interest." Such a statement might be the label some future historian will apply to our time, and he could be right. But it's also a summary of Satan's challenge to the Lord God in one of the greatest stories in religious literature, the book of Job. It leads off the wisdom section of the Old Testament, just ahead of Psalms and Proverbs.

It's a story of how a person reacts to the deaths of his children, rejection by a spouse and friends, a ravaging disease and depression. Stress? Job had it all.

The story takes place in the land of Uz (not Oz), in the pastoral landscape somewhere east of the Jordan River, in pagan or Gentile country. When it was supposed to have happened isn't clear in the book itself, and there are a lot of expert guesses, anytime from the early days of Abraham until after Judah's exile. Anyway, it happened a long time ago when life was simpler—or more complicated, if you were Job.

Whenever and wherever it was written, we're given a look at how deeply and deliberately some people thought about God and his reality back in the early days of religious inquiry. The book of Job is considered to be among the most profound in the Old Testament—or at least the hardest to unravel. The similarity to modern attitudes toward religion are startling.

The book is much more than the biography of an agribusiness tycoon who goes bankrupt and loses his family the same day. The story mirrors the life of the faithful people of Israel, suffering for their integrity, humbled often in their innocence.

There are a number of parallels to the life of Jesus, beginning with Satan's challenge to his integrity.[1] It sums up the universal human condition in one man's life, depicting the virtue of integrity over expediency. It is a parable of *true faith* in the *true grace* of the one *true God*.

The story of Job begins one celestial day when the court of heaven is in session; Satan, the "Accuser," comes before God to continue an old debate. Job was the Lord's idea of what he had in mind for humanity: The man had integrity, a generous faith, and a humble nature. Satan claimed otherwise, saying Job was a pious fraud, a man God had favored and protected from the harshness of life. Furthermore, if he lost that protection and had to face hardship like everyone else, his faith would fall apart and instead of praising, he would curse God.

So in midlife, Job goes through a valley of the darkest night. God allows Satan to abuse Job terribly, yet without touching Job's person. Raiding parties from neighboring tribes carry off his camels and donkeys, killing his herdsmen and their families. The same day a fiery lava falls from heaven and destroys his flocks and the shepherds guarding them. Worst of all, a violent storm collapses the house where his sons and daughters have gathered for a reunion, killing them all.

Job is devastated. In anguish he tears his clothes and falls on the ground. Yet even in the depths of his despair, he sees reality clearly: "Naked I came from my mother's womb, and naked shall I return there; the Lord gave, and the Lord has taken away; blessed be the name of the Lord."[2]

God points out to Satan how Job persists in his integrity despite his tragedy. "He still holds fast to his innocence although you incited me against him to ruin him without cause."[3] But Satan isn't satisfied. He reminds the Lord that he has protected Job's person. "All that people have they will give to save their lives. But stretch out your hand now and touch his bone and his flesh, and he will curse you to your face." The Lord said to Satan, "Very well, he is in your power; only spare his life."[4]

Satan goes to work on Job, who has a monumental reaction. He breaks out in boils all over his body, from the crown of his head to the soles of his feet. As he sits among the ashes of his life he scrapes and scratches at the boils with a piece of broken pot.

There is more stress to come for Job. His wife ridicules him, asks him why he still clings to his cherished integrity. What good is it to him now? How can he respect himself and this God he depends on? As low as her husband has fallen, there is yet one action he should take; she urges him to "Curse God, and die."[5]

Job's experience is the stuff of our worst nightmares. It *could* happen that in a round of corporate callousness we'd be the victims of downsizing, find ourselves laid off, and lose our income. Without employment we could use up all our savings trying to find work. And without health insurance, what would happen if we broke a leg or had a heart attack from all the stress? Worse, a car accident could wipe out the children. Would we tell ourselves we're fools to believe there is a God who cares? Would we believe that integrity, honesty, and faithfulness can mean anything anymore? Satan's aim was to derail Job's trust in God. Although his strategy may have been different with Jesus, Satan's goal was the same, as it is now with us.

News of Job's disasters flows through the camel caravans to his friends, three wise men from afar: Eliphaz of Teman; Bildad the Shuhite; and Zophar from Naamath. They agree to visit Job together to bring him sympathy and encouragement.

But when they catch sight of the scabrous wretch he has become, they are appalled and weep for him. With great ceremony, the three friends sprinkle dust on their heads and tear their robes.

Then, stunned to silence they sit with Job for seven days and seven nights.[6]

But they're thinking. They're beginning to wonder what great sin Job has committed to wind up among the ashes, his life a ruin. Their sympathies begin to take on a hard edge. Could they bless him now? Love him as a neighbor? Should they not keep a wary distance from this man who is so obviously accursed of God?

But first, Job speaks. He distances himself from himself. He curses the day he was born because he is found guilty of what? Of life? Job is hedged in by darkness. Why start such a life at all? He longs for death, but it will not come.

His soul shrinks from the outside conditions, and he does not have the spiritual energy for an inner search to see what his distress might mean. Instead, his friends tell him what it means, in long attacks on his integrity and faith.

The first to attack is Eliphaz, who asks why Job is discouraged by his calamities. Has he not understood, and even taught others, that the blameless and innocent are never ruined as he has been? Doesn't that tell him something?[7]

Eliphaz reminds Job no mortal can be righteous before God. The Lord does not trust his angels, so why should Job expect more?[8] Eliphaz urges Job to plead with God for a miracle, but only if Job is worthy.[9] For Eliphaz, it means that Job deserves his calamities, they are the discipline of God. Only if Job accepts that truth can he expect the mercy of the Lord.[10] The other two men silently agree.

Job responds in anguish, wishing God would crush him completely, it would be a relief, a joy! And his joy would be in knowing he had never consciously disobeyed the direction of the Lord and never "denied the words of the Holy One."[11] In contrast, he resents the words of Eliphaz and the tacit agreement of the others. They see his situation, and rather than give him sympathy and support, his friends are afraid for themselves because they cannot really pinpoint what he has done to deserve his calamity.

"Look at me!" Job challenges them. "Listen to what I am saying, then tell me if I'm lying to you!"[12] He points out that he is at the end of his rope, nothing worse can happen to him and he is eager to die—so why should he lie to them? What good would it do? The meaning of his life is at stake.

Distressed by the added burden Eliphaz has laid on him, Job cries out to God, "Why are you leaning so heavily on me? I am a man; like all men I have sinned, yet now you have made me a special target? I have turned from my sin, why have you not forgiven me?"[13]

Bildad leaps in at this point and peels off some more bark: Job's children are dead because of their own sin, but if Job will turn his back on his own sinful ways and become pure and upright, God will restore his wealth and position. For God does not reject a blameless person.[14]

Job agrees that God is just. But Job is beginning to think that God's justice and his own innocence aren't on the same page. It seems to him the Lord destroys both the blameless and the wicked arbitrarily.[15] Job feels he cannot reach God, cannot speak God's language in order to explain how things are for a human. Job longs for someone who can, an arbiter to speak for both sides.[16]

Job descends further into bitter despair. Given the opportunity, he would confront God: "Do not condemn me; let me know why you contend against me."[17] He asks why the Almighty Power oppresses him and favors the wicked. Is God a nitpicker that he would search for sin in Job, even though God knows he is not guilty? The Lord has shaped him like the potter shapes clay, shown him kindness and developed his spirit—then pulled the rug out from under his feet and smashed him.

Zophar reacts to Job's long complaint against God, and his claim to be innocent in God's sight.[18] Again without specifics, Zophar makes a generalized accusation and urges Job to put away his sin, because wickedness is bound to fail.

Job responds with heat, "Those at ease have contempt for misfortune." He begs them to consider nature: the birds and the fish would tell them that God has indeed done this to him, in his wisdom.[19] Job grows more offended at their nagging, and wishes they would stop talking altogether; he doesn't need their comfort, and their accusations are false.[20]

The poetry of the drama goes on, through repeated challenges by the wise men and Job's responses. Their positions harden. The friends insist his situation proves their point,

God does not bless sinners, you find God's favor with right living.[21] Job continues to insist he is innocent, and God is unjust
in his punishment. There is already a witness vouching for
him in heaven, and he will be vindicated at the end of time,
when God will stand with him for all to see.[22]

In effect Job puts God on trial,[23] protesting that the innocent suffer and God does not come to their aid. Job gives voice
to an accusation we have heard in modern terms: Why does
God allow concentration camps or ethnic cleansing? Were
only lawbreakers allowed to die in the gas chambers of Belsen
and Auschwitz? Were only evil men lined up and shot in
Kosovo? Do only sinful children die of starvation in the Sudan
or Bangladesh? In avalanches in northern Quebec or mud-
slides in Nicaragua or tornadoes through Arkansas, were sinners the sole target of God's wrath?

Job rejects his friends' shallow advice. He refuses to bribe
God with pious cover-ups; God doesn't accept kickbacks. Job
believes he sees the world in its true light—cold, impersonal,
unworthy of his integrity and faith. Stuff happens; rain falls on
the just and the unjust alike. Furthermore Job sees that some
people sail through life without God and without problems.
They pile up wealth and honors and are content with their
lives.[24] Job has honored God in his life, with his integrity, and
now he sits in utter destruction. Why? He is completely baf-
fled by the paradoxes, the puzzling inconsistencies of God's
administration.

Elihu steps in now, to set things straight in the wisdom of
his youth. Who's this Elihu? Where does he spring from?
Maybe he's in the crowd of morbid onlookers who gather at
any disaster. In any event, he has listened to the arguments of
the three friends and believes they've been too easy on Job.
He accuses Job of hypocrisy and blasphemy—who is he to

judge God and to claim innocence of sin? Elihu wields the sword of his opinion with slashing arrogance, but does little more than sum up the arguments against Job, as a district attorney sums up the state's case against a criminal.

Then God speaks.[25]

Maud read Job because she was going through her Bible from Genesis to Revelation, as if reading a novel. She liked Genesis and Exodus, full of stories and events. So when she hit Leviticus she was willing to slog through the laws and rules and commandments. "I learned stuff," she told her daughter. "But a lot of it is hard to understand." Then she hit Numbers and Deuteronomy and nearly gave up.

"Like reading the phone book," she muttered to herself. "Only the phone book has some familiar names."

Maud's courage returned when she broke into Joshua and Judges. Then she urged Stephanie to read Ruth. "It'll restore your confidence as a woman." She sailed through Samuel and Kings with enough momentum for more phone books in the Chronicles. Ezra and Nehemiah seemed a pitiful let-down from the glories of Solomon's reign; to Maud the little group resettling Jerusalem looked like children playing grown-ups, she wondered why they even tried. Then she read Esther and saw the triumph of small efforts of faith.

But Job? "It begins as if you're about to learn something life changing," Maud told Zedekiah at the next potluck. She asked him to eat with her and answer some questions. "So why can't I figure out what happened? What was it all about anyway? God comes in at the end and doesn't say a word about Job's situation or why he put him in such a spot. I'm really confused. And I don't want to be."

Zed chewed on a carrot stick, took a swallow of coffee, and put down his cup slowly. "Look at it this way, Maud. Job and his accusers argue with all the logic and reason and moral values at their command. God doesn't argue in these terms, because they are not big enough. That's the point of what you've been reading.

"Remember, God only speaks to Job, not to the others—except to tell them they have not spoken rightly as Job has.

"As for Job, God asks where he was when the Almighty built the world, organized the stars above and the seas below, and regulated the days and seasons."

Maud interrupted, "But why does God pile it on like he does? Poor Job, he was devastated."

"Aren't most of us down at one time or another?" Zed responded. "Job—and his so-called friends—have been looking at it only from his perspective, as if the universe revolved around this one man and his problems. *But halfway through God's speech, Job gets the picture. He finally sees himself against the whole of reality, and his quarrel with God is over.*"

Maud's face bespoke her confusion: "So what has he learned? What am I supposed to learn?"

Zedekiah sat quietly for a moment before he spoke. "I think he realized his ideas of God had been idols of his own making. Nothing we can imagine can put ourselves in God's mind. What we understand is from our human perspective, and we dare not try to shrink God's overview to fit ours.

"All we have to go on is what God let's us see," Zed went on. "He has shown us a great deal of what he wants us to be through the law and the prophets. The gospels tell us he even became human in Jesus, and his death becomes a monumental statement of God's character and our responsibility.

"Yet it would be a mistake to assume that what he showed

us as a human covers all there is to know of God. God in Jesus shows us only as much of God as human nature can handle. There's a limit to our perceptions, just as Job discovered."

Maud shook her head, "I don't know if I'll ever understand what you just said. What did Job learn that I can understand now?"

"Well, he learned life can have some nasty surprises," Zed grimaced. "He already knew you can't find integrity if all you live for is what you hope to squeeze out of God. Doesn't matter what happens to you in life, it's your integrity that counts. But he sees himself more clearly now against the magnified reality of God and he repents in dust and ashes."

Even in his dark valley, Job knew that his integrity was the only continuing evidence he had of the reality of God. He had no other proof of the grace of God at work in his life. Same with us. God's living presence in our lives makes itself known in the desire to live honorably, honestly, wholesomely, with patience, and concern for others. It demonstrates the quiet power of a reality other than the world of me-first, of self-promotion, and one-upmanship.

It isn't a matter of *if* we will go through a dark valley in life. The language in Job acknowledges a recurring situation, a *whenever* we go through hard times. Suffering is a part of living. Furthermore, we grow from the rough times, the times we're poorest in spirit. We grow if we'll accept the lessons they can teach us. The grace of God is always available to us; the presence and comfort of God is always there to get us through.

We can learn much from Job, who suffered even though he was a man of faith. So where is the justice? When her boss was shot, remember what Stephanie's potluck group advised her—

1. Stuff happens. Don't blame God.
2. Listen and learn—God will make sense out of nonsense.
3. Trust God and go where he takes you.

It's not an easy lesson. But to learn it is worth your life.

*I think in circles. I am thinking the same scared
thoughts as I did a year ago. I worry about not
getting anywhere and about worrying too much.
I can't decide anything, I really want to be able
to say, stop it, Peter, take a step forward
into the pretty picture, instead of one step
outward so you can look at it.*

—Peter

*My Lord God, I have no idea where I am going.
I do not see the road ahead of me. . . . But . . .
I know . . . you will lead me by the right road
though I may know nothing about it.*

—Thomas Merton

SEVEN

I Fear No Evil; for You Are with Me . . .

I had no idea what a werewolf was, or I would have stayed home and gone skating with my dog. Gosh could skate on ice as long as he didn't need to turn, then his style got messy. He tried hard, but spent too much effort getting his back end to follow his front.

My sister Anne wanted to go shopping in Winnipeg and she made it sound reasonably entertaining to a nine-year-old from the country. That winter my mother spent four months in a body cast, trying to straighten out and "freeze" an arthritic back. Primitive treatment, but not too unreasonable. Although Anne was 18 years older than I and had her own life to live, she returned home and took over for mother. She cooked the meals, ran the house, and tried to keep me occupied.

Could I go to a movie while she shopped? Sounded like an idea to me. Snack on a Cadbury chocolate bar? Getting even better. See a movie? Had to wait and see what was playing.

There was some kind of romance film at the Metropolitan and a historical drama at the Tivoli. No thanks. Two others didn't have a one o'clock matinee, so that left the Capital and

The Werewolf of London. Sounded ominous, but that was the choice or squirm through *The Farmer Takes a Wife* with some new guy named Henry Fonda, or get a history lesson in *Clive of India*. Borrrrring!

Better I should have had the history lesson or caught up on farming. Instead I learned much more than I wanted about canine teeth and a mad scientist getting hairy all over, padding around at night in a dim London fog (what else?) looking for nine-year-olds to chew on. There were only ten or so other people in the Capital that Tuesday afternoon, offering no protection in numbers.

All the science stuff at the beginning wasn't too scary, but the sound track made me nervous. You could tell something fishy was going on and worse. Bad things were about to happen. I wolfed the chocolate bar and hardly tasted it, which ought to have told me something. Then came the dark night of the great transformation—in the interest of science, of course. I knew then things were going to fall apart in a big way, including me.

So when man became beast with a lot of groans and grimaces and sprouting of fur and fangs, I slid off the seat and spent time on the floor where I couldn't be seen. Big mistake. The sound of that thing snuffling around up there became overwhelming. I finally gave up and scuttled for the lobby, to wait for Anne and relative safety.

No one likes to go through fear alone.

From experience with aggressive turkeys and hairy werewolves, I contend that fear is the greatest source of stress for a child. But a scary movie is nothing compared to the real thing, the evil of being abused by those who should love and protect the child. Only a little less frightening, although in a different way, is being misunderstood and not taken seriously. As a child, I hated my inability to express thoughts and feelings clearly. I still do. It's humiliating.

Anxiety and the anticipated humiliation it hides can stay with us all our lives. We grow up denying our terrors, burying our fears behind a "cool" exterior. Sometimes it works and we convince others we are coping with life. Yet there are times we can't even convince ourselves. Then stress has a free run at us and humiliation rears its ugly head.

I have a theory about Stephen King books and scary movies. They help us ignore the dark valleys we pass through every day, starting with the crush-hour commute. There's little wisdom in claiming we're not alarmed by the world around us. Watch the evening news, skim the headlines, listen to the drive-time talk shows; it's a deadly world we live in.

Some evils seem harder to bear than others: the murder of a loved one, a child being sexually abused, losing a spouse's love to someone else, or working for a boss who believes the only way to run a tight ship is to keep his employees afraid of losing their jobs. Anyone who isn't afraid of something out there isn't telling the truth.

Some of us fear we'll never catch up, so we dread the deadlines tomorrow will bring. We're scared of more technological change when we're already behind the curve. We're afraid our co-workers will find out we're working beyond our abilities. We endure gut-eating anxiety for our family's security, because jobs like ours have been phased out, and we're too old to change.

Fear isn't reserved for nine-year-olds.

Most of us believe reality is what we face after the alarm clock goes off. Yet that kind of reality is only the tip of the iceberg lying in wait for us, as Job discovered. But, unlike Job, who has time to sit around in sackcloth and ashes, arguing with God? So we start every morning as if we're used to the world we live in, more or less. We put on a brave front and try to fool ourselves into thinking we're in control.

We push our fears into the background of our lives where they build a backlog of unruly stress, hiding its threats below the surface of our lives. We didn't buy a ticket on the *Titanic*, but the iceberg of fear is out there, lurking in the werewolf's fog.

Jesus had a revealing thing to say about the iceberg: fear inhibits freedom. He knew nasty things are out there, but he also knew that by the grace of God they cannot touch our inner core[1]—even when we are crunched by circumstances and the pressures of our responsibilities.

I fear no evil; for you are with me. . . .

Somehow faith makes it possible to live through our fears, not because we "have faith" or the threats we face aren't real, but because faith connects us with a much greater reality beyond the terrors we wake up to every morning.

Jesus knew the strengthening, sustaining, and comforting presence of God in his life. And Jesus insisted this self-same Spirit of his Father can be ours also; the Comforter and Advocate welling up in us to transform our lives.[2] His presence, his Spirit, will bring meaning to whatever we're going through and show us the way to integrity. Even when we fear that our weaknesses will betray us, as they may have done in the past, his grace will give us all we need to go from weakness to strength.[3]

In the experience of a great many people of faith, no evil can overwhelm the grace-full power of God. Neither hardship nor distress, persecution nor famine, utter poverty nor the terrors of lawlessness and war, *and not even life itself,* with all its potholes and illusions and catastrophes, can come between us and God and his love for us. If Jesus demonstrated nothing else, he showed us the love of God for people in all their life-worn struggles.[4]

People of faith have proven to themselves that fear and anxiety are flashbacks, remnants of an old slavery and its wants. But they also confirm Paul's statement that "all who are led by the Spirit of God are children of God"[5] and are free of the power of other masters. When the spirit of the world pushes its claims on us, the Spirit of God gives us the strength of his integrity. No situation can overwhelm us when the Shepherd is with us, showing us the way to escape its pressures.[6]

Our personal sufferings take on a new dimension, because in them we discover more of the grace of God than we believed possible. We go into an experience of pain and anguish to find that God has not abandoned us at all but instead is making his compassion abundantly available.

Stephanie could not feel compassion in her job at the convenience store. For months all she wanted was revenge on the man who killed her boss; it became a dark cloud of evil enveloping her life. She checked every man who came in the store against her memory: How would he look with a stocking cap over his face? And behind every woman customer who came in the door, she looked for a car with the killer in it.

She invented dramas with herself in the leading role. He

would come in, not thinking she would recognize him. But his walk, his voice, his guilt would give him away and she would know without a doubt, this was the man. She would tell her co-worker she was taking a break, then go into the stockroom and call the police.

Stephanie's fantasy expanded. She would pick up the pot of heated water kept for making hot chocolate, walk behind the man, pretend to stumble and splash it down his pants, and cripple him. Or she would run out when the police came and tell them he was armed, then the cops would have to shoot him again and again until he was dead. Or, best of all her day-dreams of vengeance, when he used his gun to threaten her, she would scream so loud he would turn to run out, trip on a floor display, and shoot himself. As he lay bleeding and in agony she would take her time calling the emergency squad and he would die on the way to the hospital.

In mid-fantasy one night, as she tidied up and refilled the condiment jars at the hot-dog cooker, she squeezed a ketchup bottle too hard in her fury. It sputtered ketchup all over her uniform and as she swiped at the blobs with her hands, she saw herself covered in his blood.

"No. This is not what I want," she told herself with sudden insight. "I want him to get caught, but I don't want to be his killer. Then he would have killed me, too." She believes it was her Shepherd showing her the way: "It was almost as if he spoke to me, and the feeling of peace and freedom came like a drink of clear water."

Stephanie had been made to understand what revenge would cost her for the rest of her life. It was enough to break the hold of a fear-filled existence, enough to set her free to become the person she could become.

Life is full of experiences to learn by, some of them as

frightening as Stephanie's. If we can see through the pain and distress, we can find the presence of God and the edge of his reality to cling to. *I fear no evil; for you are with me. . . .*

~

We need the Shepherd's presence with us, otherwise fear and despair can lock us up inside our own souls, never to let us into the open air again. Losing a child to disease, undergoing cancer's agony, or being shattered in a car accident can drain our inner and material resources to point zero. Sometimes it seems better not to live.

Death may seem a blessed relief, a way out of the pain of living. Yet death or dying closes the door on experience and growth. In times of despair, faith squeezes all there is out of life until there is nothing left but hope.

The strange, mind-scrambling new life God bestowed on Jesus broke the pattern of death and the power of fear. Then and now, practical wisdom says there is no such thing as restoring life to a decaying body. Yet the wisdom of the new perspective of *What Is* says, "There is more to reality than death. There is a much larger life we can live, and death does not spell termination."

At the end, Jesus had nothing left but hope. The enemies that lurk in human nature put him in a dreadful bind—either deny all he believed God was doing to open up his kingdom, his reality—or die. Deny or die, a choice he struggled with as the inevitable day approached. Every step he took alienated him from the religious leaders who saw him as a threat to their established ideas of God's reign. But he kept on, even in the face of his own doubts.

And he had doubts. Like the rest of us, he carried his own inner enemies too. Did he fear death? If he did not, he wasn't human like the rest of us. His friends were nearby as he grappled with those enemies, and they remembered.[7] As he hung dying, Mark reported the final doubts of Jesus, "My God, my God, why have you forsaken me?"[8] Had he been so wrong? Was this deadly pain the end result of a huge misunderstanding of the reality of God?

At that moment, the human way of understanding death and life, tragedy and comedy and all things in between, gave way to a new perspective.

As far back in history as we can go, there has been speculation about the meaning of life and the values of death. The two are inextricably tied together. If there's no meaning to life itself, then death simply puts an end to it, and God is but another figment of our imagination. But if life does have meaning, then death must be our graduation to what-comes-next. It is an evil we need no longer fear, because God is ever with us.

After his death, it took a while for the followers of Jesus to survive their grief and make sense of his life among them. They met together in their houses and talked, recalling bits and pieces of their experience with Jesus. One remembered what he said to the crowd on the beach as he spoke to them from a boat in the Sea of Galilee.[9] Another told the story of the Canaanite woman who wanted Jesus to heal her daughter.[10] Someone else recalled the events leading up to Jesus' trial and crucifixion. And they talked about the mystery of the resurrection.

Biblical scholars have not settled among themselves the puzzles about the resurrection accounts in the Gospels. Some insist they all happened just as written, and any seeming contradictions can be explained. Others insist contradictions simply don't matter since the accounts are to be interpreted as out-here, everyday words describing in-here, *What Is* experiences.

The earliest Gospel, Mark, has the least to say about the resurrection of Jesus; the latest Gospel, John, has the most. Some argue the differences between Mark and John prove that what really happened is hidden under a lot of illusion and embroidery. That might be true if we were dealing with the kind of reality engineers and auto mechanics have to live with. But we aren't. Not even stress, common as it is, can be described with clarity because one person's stress can be another's stimulation.

Even more difficult to pin down in words are the experiences of faith. I know with certainty that God IS, because the times his presence has brought new meaning and structure to my life are too numerous for me to question them. But my experiences are different from anyone else's. I can try to explain them to you, and you may have some similar events to describe, but precise words will fail us both.

Yet there is no denying the reality of our experiences. We can only measure them against the accumulated understandings of others—including the meaning of the Gospels and the resurrection.

Several women go to where Jesus was buried and find the tomb empty.[11] They see angels, who tell them Jesus has been raised from the dead. Later, one of the women, Mary of Magdala, sees a man outside the tomb. She thinks he is the gardener until she recognizes the voice of Jesus and falls at his feet.[12]

A number of the disciples are hiding from the authorities behind locked doors. Suddenly Jesus stands among them. He shows them the wounds on his body, and speaks: "Peace be with you." He even eats with them, and affirms that body and soul are a package.[13] Thomas can't believe what the others tell him, so he has his own meeting with Jesus. Then Jesus rebukes Thomas, "You became a believer because you saw me. Blest are they who have not seen as you have seen, yet who believed."[14]

A couple walking home to Emmaus meet a stranger who explains why their hopes for a leader to redeem Israel were inadequate. Their hearts are encouraged as they listen, and when they arrive home, they invite the stranger to eat with them. He doesn't have the recognizable body Thomas demanded to see, so it is only as the stranger breaks bread with them do they realize they have met the resurrected Jesus.[15]

These encounters with the resurrected Jesus were different enough from each other to tell us something we need to understand: The other side of reality can make itself known in ways so personally suited to our needs that it will change our lives forever.

Later, Paul, the man who is to become the most influential builder-of-the-faith community, meets the risen Jesus on the road to Damascus, not an embodied Jesus, but a voice and a calling and a presence so powerful it is to dominate Paul's life from that moment on.[16]

God is with us; don't ask me how it's done. In some remarkable way he lives in his people, for his people, and through his people. Over the centuries, both before and after Jesus Christ, the Spirit of God has made himself present if in no other way than in enabling us to say: *I fear no evil; for you are with me. . . .*

I have been blessed with parents that never put any doubt in my mind that I could do or be anything I wanted. . . . I hope for greater faith in God, a stable family life, devoted love, a satisfying career, greater understanding of other peoples by traveling, and possibly living for an extended period abroad. I can hope for these things because I was born in a free and rich land. I'm trying not to forget that.
—Larissa

My child, do not despise the Lord's discipline or be weary of his reproof,
for the Lord reproves the one he loves.—Proverbs

EIGHT

Your Rod and Your Staff— They Comfort Me . . .

Bread and butter and brown sugar sandwiches, wrapped in a cloth under my pillow. Not exactly health food, but this was the early '30s and food of any kind was pretty precious. My mother left the sandwiches there "to keep a fellow till breakfast" while the rest of the family slept.

Sunday breakfasts were always a little bit late, the one day Mother could sleep in. Not like weekdays. During the week a five-year-old got accustomed to waking in the winter dark with the stove lid clanging, soft wordless voices, and that hurry-up feeling that it was already late.

But not on Sundays. The house slept on, stirring and creaking and ticking and dreaming. Its soft breath lay warm against the cold high song of the power lines outside.

As the light crept into the room, I'd reach under the pillow and pull out the package. One morning a mouse, attracted by the bread, ran across my shoulder and nearly died of fright when I twitched.

It was too cold to get up until the stove was lit. One night

I left some water for the mouse in a small bowl on my bureau. During the night it froze and the bowl cracked.

Once I saw a small painted nail stuck in the wall and the shadow where a picture had hung; I wondered what it had looked like. One Sunday morning I drew a picture of our white cow on a page from my "scribbler" and speared it on the nail. Another Sunday I used crayons and drew a fishing boat on the river.

I don't remember resenting my parents or being bored. Life simply included quiet early Sunday mornings when it was too cold to get out of bed. I look back on those mornings as islands of tranquillity, when I could enjoy the safety and comfort of belonging. I was being taught a great lesson, that within such limitations one can find peace and joy and contentment. I wish I had learned the lesson better than I did.

Your rod and your staff— they comfort me . . .

Discipline isn't in the same league as child abuse. My parents never knocked me around in a rage, but I was disciplined. My father would offer a choice, smarten up and do right or risk a "swift kick in the pants." Mother's rebuke might be accompanied with a rap of a finger on my head, much the worse if it included a thimble. But I never feared being maimed.

Always, the reproaches of my parents were quick means of redirecting my life from wrong to right. It didn't always work, but over the years I learned enough self-regulating behavior to keep me out of jail. So far.

Civilizing a child is a demanding chore. Some argue for the freedom of the child to grow up as she chooses; for them "civilizing" is a bad word meaning repression. Yet appropriate discipline is as important as food and water. If we learn to accept limits as a child, we can benefit from the rigors and dis-ciplines we'll face in school and beyond.

~

Some biblical scholars consider the rod to be a long piece of tough wood used to defend against predators and helpful as a temporary barrier wedged between rocks in a rock fence. The staff, perhaps a straight tree limb with a stub of branch at the end, would be used to push or pull a sheep from the flock for special attention such as help in lambing or the treatment of a wound. Other scholars think that "rod and staff" describes just one piece of equipment the shepherd would use for both purposes: protection and direction.

Sheep may or may not be grateful for their shepherd's care, but the writer of Psalm 23 knew enough to find comfort in the rod and staff the Good Shepherd wielded for his benefit. He knew the Lord God protects *and* directs.

Protects? What about all the innocent lives lost every year through accident or disease or war on the streets? Where was the Lord God then? Out to lunch?

Ask Job; he discovered a pretty good answer. His story tells us, "Bad things happen; don't blame God. Instead, listen and learn from those experiences. And all the while, trust God and follow where he takes us."

I know there have been times when I should have been squashed like a bug on a windshield, but by the grace of God the experiences turned into lessons to live by. Last Thanksgiving, Norma and I visited with our daughter, Debby, her husband, Sam, and their girls, Megan and Dede. Sunday we headed home on the Interstate, going with the flow in the right-hand lane. Both lanes were filling up with heavy traffic as it got later in the morning. We came up behind a slow moving motor home and I watched for a chance to pass; a green sedan shot by, with a gap in behind. I pulled out and passed, and a moment later noticed a car in the right lane several lengths ahead putting on the brakes. Our only warning.

A fraction of a second later the green sedan smashed into the back of the car in front. By the grace of God I had a heartbeat to swerve left onto the grassy shoulder. Immediately ahead another car sat on the shoulder, with just enough space for us to shoot between it and the cars in the lane. As far as I could see, traffic was either moving at a crawl or stopped; we were back at the pileup end. Behind, I caught a mirror-glimpse of other cars swinging onto the shoulder.

If we hadn't had a warning brake light, if we would have been tailgating the car in front, if the shoulder had not been open and flat, if there hadn't been room to pass the stopped car on the shoulder, we might have all been doomed.

An opportunity for discipline? Yes indeed, my driving practices are still benefiting from that experience. *Your rod and your staff— they comfort me . . .*

I can use all the protection I can get, it's a dangerous world out there. But in spite of traffic and other threats to life and limb, the greatest danger I face is from myself, because I find it too easy to ignore the disciplines I need to become a truly whole person, disciplined to integrity and virtue as well as calling or vocation.

Not many of us like discipline, unless it's for something we want to achieve. An athlete will work long hours to develop the skills and coordination necessary to excel in a given sport. A musician exercises constantly in order to perfect her competence. A physician must "practice" throughout a career in medicine. Any work of any merit takes training and directed action of the right kind, or it doesn't measure up.

But there's more to life than competence and rigorously trained skills. I can push for my place in the sun yet miss becoming the person God intended me to be, miss the fullness of life God would lead me to live. Existence involves what I do, who I am, and what I am becoming. Too easily I can ignore the disciplined process of maturing in God's way—the *only* way that can give me a meaningful answer to the great questions of existence: What am I? Why am I here? Where am I going?

It isn't a matter of religious correctness. For some people religion means getting their doctrines and beliefs on straight, like a suit of clothes, and having done so, that's all that life requires. As Jesus pointed out, many of the religiously correct people he knew were so wrapped up in the laws and politics of their faith that they missed out on mercy and compassion. What they believed didn't allow for the grace of God to continue its work in their own lives; they lived as if they had already arrived and had no need for repentance and redirection.[1] Yet according to Jesus, true recruits for the reality of God find themselves involved in a continual process of refining and maturing throughout their days.[2]

It isn't a matter of religious feelings either. For some people religion means getting happy, praising God, enjoying the free release of their emotions. Good stuff, but feelings can be as superficial as doctrinal correctness, according to Jesus.[3] Participation in the realm of God, in the reality of *What Is*, takes more than getting into our feelings or understanding doctrines correctly.

Does this begin to sound too complicated? It isn't. Jesus found it distressing that his listeners could not grasp the sim-

plicity of his message. Even biblical scholars missed the point.⁴
But the psalmist who wrote "I fear no evil" knew what was
required. While he lived out his beliefs and expressed his feelings, there was something else that gave him comfort and
assurance; he could trust the continuing discipline of the
Lord, his Shepherd, to give his life meaning and direction and
contentment.

The discipline of God requires only that we be willing to
be redirected—he will do the directing. That's repentance. It
requires our commitment to follow as God takes us step by
step through the process of being "made a new creation in
Christ."⁵ We repent, God redirects. We commit, with God's
grace we mature. It's a transaction between our faith and
God's grace.

The Bible gives us a classic example of this in the
rearrangement of the life of Saul of Tarsus. Back then, if you
drew a line north from Jerusalem, past Damascus and up
through Syria to Antioch where the Mediterranean coastline
hangs a left, there's Tarsus, just around the corner to the west.
It was a major hub of trade for the inland provinces over the
mountains to the north. Tarsus had become a free city-state of
the Roman Empire and a university center on a par with the
great cities of Alexandria and Athens. At Tarsus, Cleopatra
paid a call on Marc Antony in 38 B.C.

Many of the residents of Tarsus were granted Roman citi-
zenship, and this coveted privilege was passed to their children. This was the case for Saul, born in Tarsus both a Roman
and a Jew, who later studied under Gamaliel, perhaps the
leading scholar and rabbi in Jerusalem.⁶

Probably at age 30, Saul became a rabbi himself and a prosecutor for the Sanhedrin, the religious and political council of Israel. He became a terror to the early followers of Jesus, then known as a Jewish sect called The Way. The followers of The Way did not yet call themselves Christians; that name came later to the mixed bag of believers in Antioch,[7] up near Tarsus.

Back then in Jerusalem, the disciples of Jesus still counted themselves Jews of the covenant of Abraham, renewed under Moses and enriched through the prophets of old. A problem simmered to the surface when the Greek-speaking followers of The Way felt overlooked and underrated by the local believers. Finally their widows complained they were being treated unfairly in the distribution of food. Seven Greek-speaking Jews, all with Greek names, were appointed as adjunct apostles, and charged with the responsibility to look after practical matters.[8]

Among them were Philip and Stephen. Philip preached the gospel to the Samaritans and also baptized the first Gentile, a court official of Queen Candace of Ethiopia.[9] Stephen worked among the Greek-speaking Jews and drew the ire of some who accused him of blasphemy before the council of the Sanhedrin. Stephen responded by accusing the council of a huge error in killing Jesus. As they raged at him, Stephen told them he saw Jesus. "Look," he said, "I see the heavens opened and the Son of Man standing at the right hand of God."

Stephen was abruptly stoned to death. The executioners took off their coats and laid them at the feet of Saul, defender of the faith.[10]

"Indeed," Saul explained later, "I myself was convinced that I ought to do many things against the name of Jesus of Nazareth. And that is what I did in Jerusalem; with authority received from the chief priests, I not only locked up many of the saints in prison, but I also cast my vote against them when they were being condemned to death."[11]

Later, Saul asked for letters of authority from the chief priests to go to Damascus in pursuit of followers of The Way. On this journey, all his training as a Pharisee, all his relentless energy, all his commitment to the God of his forefathers, indeed his entire direction in life was turned around: *He met Jesus.* It became the turning point of his life, a story he told again and again wherever he went.[12]

Paul never forgot his persecution of the church. Although he became the apostle to the Gentile world, he carried the memory of his deadly attacks on The Way. "For I am the least of the apostles, unfit to be called an apostle, because I persecuted the church of God."[13] Nevertheless, his repentance was genuine and thorough. He never repented of being a Jew, he simply gave himself over to a new mission in Christ, a mission to the Gentiles.

But wait! Saul didn't repent, turn around, and reform his life until after God knocked him to the ground, right? So it was God's action, not Saul's?

Let's say it was call-response. God had been calling him for a long time, only Saul hadn't been paying attention. All the things he learned about the reality of God under Gamaliel had been speaking to Saul. What he heard about The Way as he went about his persecution of the followers of Jesus spoke to him. The look on the face of Stephen as he died under the stones thrown by the mob haunted him. By the time he was blinded by the light on the way to Damascus, Saul was more than ready to say, "What am I to do, Lord?"[14]

All of us have experiences when the light beckons us out of our darkness. Some of us just take longer to respond than others. And some—too full of themselves and the world around them to see or hear the reality of God and accept his disciplined life—never respond.

Many of us don't see the need for "spiritual" discipline. Even more, *we don't see the need for interference in who we are.* Don't meddle with my head or my being; my personality is off-limits to anyone else. Who I am is who I am; we take it as the most basic human right. It's a proud position to assume and puts us right up there with God. Independence of God seems a brave, grown-up thing to reach for, but—if we're honest in our research of spiritual history—we also have to assume it may be ruinous and degrading and ultimately foolish.

Instead, what if the most basic human right includes access to the grace to become a more complete, fulfilled human being? *Even more than we thought to become?* As "becoming-whole persons" we can be much more than simply the sum of parts that classify and define us when we allow God to discipline who we are becoming.

When Jesus declared the *What Is* of God was here, within reach of faith, he urged his hearers to change their direction, repent, and undergo a reformation of their point of view.[15] What was it he had in mind? Am I to repent of my sins so I may become right with God? Is the discipline of God akin to giving up something for Lent? It can't be a bad idea to turn away from envy or pride or lust or any other of the deadly transgressions.[16]

But this would be a less than adequate approach to a more extensive need. We really do not know what we can become, because we haven't gotten there yet. So we do not know how to discipline ourselves in order to get there. If we knew, we could at least make plans and forecasts: If I study art, I will become an artist. But we do not know what it will take to become the mature person God has in mind. We have no idea what our future could be until we allow God's discipline to shape it.

Until we do, we are going to experience stresses we won't fully understand. But when we do, we'll know what the psalmist meant, *Your rod and your staff—they comfort me* . . .

*My generation's problems started with population
growth and using up the earth's resources faster
than she could replace them. Our age group
was filled with bright students aware of the problems
and headed toward fighting them, so there is hope
and lots of it. But there are way too many kids
who don't want to be a part of the solution. . . .
Basically I intend to live each day to its absolute
fullest, while remembering that I hope to have a
positive impact on my world.*

—Natasha

~

*When we're up to our armpits in alligators,
it's hard to remember we're supposed
to be cleaning the swamp.*

—Graffiti

NINE

You Prepare a Table Before Me in the Presence of My Enemies . . .

I t may have been a five-year-old's rebellion against the golden rule or a test of size versus surprise. Certainly we do not hurt other people merely out of curiosity.

But I was curious. What if big people were not so big? Say, just my height?

Out behind our house, my big brothers had dug a huge hole and lowered into it a monstrous wood-fired steam boiler to heat the woolen mill buildings; it got viciously cold in Manitoba winters. I was appalled and fascinated at the same time by the beast in the basement.

I badgered my father, could I please go down and watch it being loaded? The week before my fifth birthday Alf MacKay, who looked after the boiler and washed the wool in big warm-water vats in the washhouse, carried me down the ten-foot ladder and sat me at a safe distance from the fire door.

I watched in stricken wonder as he swung the big door

open. The inferno inside blew blasts of flame as Alf threw in four-foot cordwood logs. He mixed poplar and Manitoba maple and willow until the firebox was full. Alf noticed my keen interest; he took my hand and drew me closer and knelt down to show me the draft regulator and the ash door, the water and steam gauges with their quivering needles. Great mysteries!

All that week I watched whenever Alf climbed down in the pit to check the gauges and feed the boiler more logs. I begged him to take me down with him again, but I think my mother had asked him not to. So I sat or knelt in the snow at the top of the ladder until his face would rise up at the top of the ladder at just about my height.

On my birthday, Mother dressed me to go with her to Selkirk, so I wasn't to kneel in the snow or sit, but I could watch Alf MacKay feed the boiler. I ran out to watch him throw cordwood down into the pit and told him I was five. And did I look any bigger? He thought maybe a little. But not much. He stepped through the hatchway onto the top of the ladder and sank down past my eyes. His big smile was only inches from my face.

I've often wondered why I hit him on the nose with a little fist. Alf's eyes blinked and he nearly fell all the way to the bottom of the ladder. But only his feet slipped; he held onto the ladder and his face came back up fast, blood running from his nose. He scooped me up and ran for the house and banged on the door. Mother took one look at Alf and brought him in, listening to what had happened. She sat me in a corner with a look and held a damp cloth to Alf's nose.

With a few choice words Mother made me to understand I had taken advantage of Alf's friendship and hurt his nose. It was wrong to do so. For a week I would not be allowed to watch him feed the boiler and then I would have to ask *his* permission, every time. And I was to apologize for my behavior. Now.

Why are kids little monsters sometimes? Why do otherwise decent people turn into sociopaths when they get behind the wheel of a car? We do not know the reason bad behavior shows up in unexpected places. For all we know about human nature, we are as yet babes in our understanding of evil and its causes.

My enemies are legion, and so close they go with me wherever I go, sit down with me at every meal. Often it is indifference to another's well-being, or the fear of becoming involved in someone else's troubles. I'm good at self-justification and putting a spin on events so I come off looking better than I should. And I can covet my neighbor's affluence, then go out and buy the objects I covet with a credit card I can't afford.

Look at the other enemies we carry with us. If the media measures us with any accuracy, we're never far from sexual misbehavior. Arrogance and pride dominate our relationships when feelings of racial, national, and spiritual superiority take over. The malice and anger we consider "righteous indignation" boils to the surface in letters to the editor or savage voices on the call-in shows.

How about simple gluttony? Is it so simple to lose weight, quit smoking, or give up our drug of choice? Stephanie has proof that losing weight is the greatest problem in the world, worse than taxes, old age, or tooth plaque. She told their Bible-study group you can count on it, every women's magazine in her convenience store will offer a new way to peel off the pounds. "The only other stories they carry as often are on how to have better sex. With anybody."

Stephanie's mother Maud added, "And every new diet plan has a coupon beside it for a cake mix or frozen dessert— only 600 calories a spoonful."

Last time they met, the potluck group decided to study Paul's letter to the Christians in Rome, starting with the first two chapters. Maud was puzzled about Paul's ideas on human nature.

"He sure pushes us all into the same boat," Maud complained. "There aren't any decent people among us, only gossips, gluttons, and murderers. What's his problem, Zedekiah?"

Zed looked around the group, most of whom were nodding in sympathy with Maud. It was Dino who responded first; the bike messenger was sitting beside Stephanie again. "I think Paul's setting the background, that's all," Dino asserted. "We never see ourselves as evil people. We see ourselves as better than that—and Paul won't let us get away with it."

Zed nodded. "Dino's right. Paul builds a solid case that every human has done evil of some kind, sometime, and isn't anywhere near the image of God. As he puts it, we fall far short of the glory of God, all of us."

Maud muttered, "Like Pogo in the old comics I used to read as a kid. We've met the enemy and he is us."

"You got it," Zed agreed. "We know better. We've always known better. We choose to go our own way, and not listen to God. It's part of the freedom God gives us because he wants our free and willing response. So even good people do bad things—because we choose to. "

The enemies we create in ourselves shrug off the God-who-would-help-us. We cannot imagine he might know us better than we do ourselves, and that he might have a better direction for our lives than anything we can come up with on our own. We refuse his help because we don't see the need for it.

And even though we may be committed to the integrity of God, there is something about us that resonates to evil. Too often the enemy within responds to the enemy in others. The idea of "evil forces" in the world may seem a dated superstition, but only if we're willing to ignore the reality of hate groups, "ethnic cleansing," and religious intolerance—and those times in our own lives when we have chosen to hurt others. Then we have ourselves become a force for evil.

The letter Paul wrote to the Christians at Ephesus is different from his others. Ephesians provides new insights into Paul's spiritual chemistry and his maturing and deepening understanding of the *What Is* of God. Like Jesus, he always tried to explain in everyday terms the reality of God's realm. That's a tough job, especially when we prefer to think in terms of what we can work out to our benefit.

Paul had plenty of flesh and blood enemies. In the town of Lystra he had been stoned like Stephen;[1] at Philippi in Macedonia he was beaten with rods and jailed,[2] in Jerusalem a mob tried to kill him.[3]

After that Paul spent most of the rest of his life in prison for his faith, in Caesarea and in Rome. Paul made human enemies, yet the greater threat he perceived came from "principalities and powers." As he told the Ephesians, "Our struggle is not against enemies of blood and flesh, but . . . against the cosmic powers of this present darkness."[4]

The cosmic powers of *this* present darkness wouldn't surprise Paul. He might not recognize the political structures today, but he'd not be surprised by some of today's political maneuvering.

Human nature stays the same, even though the tactics might change. We know how to push the right buttons to bring out the worst in each other. And now from one side of the world to the other, we can release more malice and do it faster than ever before. We're running out of time, in more ways than one.

"Ladies and gentlemen, it's going to work." A gleam of triumph accented his calm statement as Satan laid his pen on the mahogany conference table, placing it neatly, precisely, beside the portfolio of memoranda.

"The system has been in the experimental stage with continuing success for over four decades, which is ample time to prove its worth."

There were 20 others seated around the huge round table, strong personalities reflecting their leader's confidence in them. One in a soot-colored suit, leaned forward. "Sir, a question."

"Yes, Daemon?"

Daemon swung his glasses in his fingers. "Is the system more effective than our older, proven methods?"

"I am convinced that it is," Satan responded. "Turn to schedule three in your memoranda for some up-to-the-moment comparisons.

"Notice item two. In primitive circumstances we used primitive methods. Persecution was often effective within families, particularly the threat of being torn apart by lions. Many a parent with small children could face anything but the prospect of their little ones being ripped to pieces by wild beasts.

"But threats of violence, even of gas chambers and firing

squads, produced a poor grade of recruit. There was always the need to reinforce the pressure, which took a great deal of time and effort. While it remains a useful tool in some backward cultures, we are achieving much more cost-effective results with the new method."

Satan paused and smiled at his committee. "We take away time; that's all there is to it. A ridiculously simple tactic; but simple things are often more productive. My friends, it's the biggest steal in history!"

"Think of it!" he continued. "We've built the better mousetrap. We have industries and businesses everywhere demanding more work and longer hours from their employees. To anyone with a moment to spare, we have given something more to do. By banishing peaceful moments—moments previously given to introspection and contemplation—we have done what no amount of persecution has been able to do before."

He gestured to the woman on his right. "I'll let Mata Harriman speak from her research."

The exquisitely attired Harriman glanced at her notes, cleared her throat, and then began. "The steep increase in tension and irritability has been most gratifying. Such elements as integrity and honor have been weakened and are no longer considered important. Court dockets are overflowing, causing justice to give way to plea-bargaining. But the most significant result our people have noted is the steep decline in attempts at prayer. Busy people simply have no time for it."

Harriman smiled at the faces around the table. "Even when someone does pray, it's hurried, fragmentary—and meaningless; there's no heart to it. Furthermore, the so-called believer loses interest in what our enemy calls 'spiritual matters.' He has no time to listen for the 'still, small voice of' . . .

"She hesitated, and a number of indrawn breaths confirmed that she was about to speak the dreadful name. She went on firmly, "He no longer can hear the voice of . . . God."

Satan spoke now. "Our aim is to stimulate the people so they are slightly behind in everything, never quite finished before they must start in on something new. When people do have a moment, we've got them flipping through a couple hundred channels on television, browsing the Internet, talking on a cell phone, or listening to one of those how-to-get-rich-quick tapes."

"Devilishly clever, sir."

"Thank you, Daemon. The general effect is remarkable. Our subjects quickly adapt to the hope of getting ahead some day, and we find we can actually step up the pace at this stage. Especially for the young." He nodded for Mata Harriman to continue.

"Here is where delicate skill must come into play." She held up a chart and pointed to the steady rise in pressure along a time line. "We must not pile on too much at once. Just enough and no more. Too much breaks the suckers—I'm sorry—the subject's unrealistic optimism, and we must start again." She folded the chart and slipped it into a file on the table.

"Thank you, Mata." Satan scanned the faces around the table. "Any more questions? No? Then remember our new approach. Encourage your people to steal time! Go out there and find new ways to do it better!

"That's all for tonight. Keep up the bad work."

So much of our stress is over time, and finding enough of it to accomplish all we want—to be with the kids, do our work, fight traffic, get enough sleep, and be somebody. There are moments we're proud of our busyness; it proves we're alive or important or at least like everyone else in our misery. Always to be on the run becomes a way of life and we don't know what to do about it, or even if we want to.

"But my boss has control of most of my time," we say. "If I don't put in the extra hours he demands, I'll get passed over for promotion."

I'd like to blame someone else, anyone else for the time pressures on my life, but too many of the decisions I continue to make generate their own kind of problems and bring their own brand of stress and anxiety. Whenever I wise up, whenever I begin to ask God to help me make better decisions, then time seems to ease its pressures and I begin to get my life back.

The continuing value of the Bible is its ability to hold up a mirror so we can see ourselves clearly. From beginning to end, the Bible deals with the human failure to understand *What Is*. We have eyes to see but we can't see, ears to hear but we often choose to listen to something else instead.[5]

Born with the impulse to mature into the image of God, we are also born with the freedom to reject that high calling.

So we reject the possibility of a greater self that goes beyond our lesser self. We refuse the gift and the giver, and cannot grow any more than we are, and so miss out on the grace of *What Is*.

You prepare a table before me in the presence of my enemies . . .
Even in our freedom to ignore him, God loves us,[6] not for what we've done or neglected to do in the past, but for what we could become in his grace.[7] Jesus pointed out that God

welcomes all who come to him in hope of something better in their lives,[8] if only to gain some relief from those deadly enemies within.

The power of God's grace can reach into where we live, in the midst of our enemies, and feed us all the strength we need to turn from self-destruction to a life of freedom and peace. Jesus became a living demonstration of the power of God to lift us out of what was into *What Is*, and a new beginning.

In the maelstrom of an overly busy life, "when we're up to our armpits in alligators," God sets a table for us. Not to congratulate us for who we are and celebrate the mess we've made of our lives, but so we may "eat" what he has for us and discover the grace and peace of his way, to eat of the fullness of life he has prepared for us.

I have to remind myself it's all right to sit at his table with my own particular host of enemies. That's who I am, and the Shepherd has prepared a table for me too. I keep reminding myself to eat what he sets before me day by day, to take comfort in the disciplines of his rod and staff, and to watch for the transforming miracle of his grace to emerge as he calls me to his purpose.

I will name the enemies I sit among, and by the grace of God, I will have nothing more to do with them. Yet, like always, I'll bump up against some tough decisions and make some more mistakes, create some more enemies, but if I continue to be willing to live in God's reality, my life will take on more of his reality in me. The life he rolls out ahead for me will be a new creation, always. And a new peace will come sit with me.

The God of *What Is* knows the human condition intimately. We are created in his image to survive all the complex problems of life while maturing in his grace. It will be our only real achievement.

Such a maturing process is always available to us, but it isn't automatic. Stress and anxiety and indecision come as we move into the next difficulty, the next challenge, up against the next enemy. And stress will ease as we learn anew how to live by God's grace in that new situation.

We're always surrounded by problems, by stresses, by "enemies." Yet the table of the Lord God is always there, spread before us, with all the nourishment we need to live with his strength and peace.

It's interesting how after all our hemming and hawing it's the simplest things we worry about: I fear failure to provide for my family. I hope to live a life, then die a death that is in balance with that life. Christianity is a set of tools to use, like other religions. Christianity is mine, I've invested in its symbols.

—Joshua

Let us be bread, blessed by the Lord, broken and shared, life for the world. Let us be wine, love freely poured. Let us be one in the Lord.

—Thomas J. Porter

• TEN •

You Anoint My Head with Oil; My Cup Overflows . . .

P salm 23 describes the abundant grace of God in terms of ancient Middle Eastern hospitality, a hospitality which defined the relationship of host and guest. When a prominent herdsman wished to honor a neighbor or friend or visiting tribal leader, he would prepare a banquet, call others to eat with him, and seat the esteemed guest at his right hand at the table. It would be a feast of generous proportions, the more lavish, the more honor to the guest.

If the guest's enemies were invited, the host expected from them courtesy and respect for the guest. If the host were then to anoint the head of the guest and fill his cup to overflowing, a further relationship would be established. The guest now moved under the protection and favor of the host and all of the host's resources were made available to him. The guest's enemies became the host's enemies, his friend's became the host's friends.

The Greek term, Christ, means "the anointed of God." When Jesus was baptized by John the Baptist in the Jordan,

John saw the Spirit of God descend on Jesus and heard a voice say, "You are my beloved Son; with you I am well pleased."[1] The gospels teach that in the anointing of Jesus, all his friends and followers were gathered into the same relationship he enjoyed with his Father. When we eat with him at God's table, we come under the protection and favor of our faithful Lord.

The rituals of eating meals together with others have meanings far beyond the function of nutrition.

No matter the work we do, when lunchtime rolls around, a lot of us will take our brown bag and find somebody to eat with. It's a human thing; there is something about eating a meal that demands companionship and socializing. "Found these jeans at a yard sale Saturday; only four dollars. Fit better than the last pair I bought new." "What'll you do if we get laid off next month?" "Thanks for the pickle. Have some tapioca pudding?"

My big brother, Hugh John, hated tapioca, wouldn't eat it if you begged him to. And he thought eating tapioca pudding made with water instead of milk was worse than chewing up a mess of frog's egg—cold frog's eggs.

Hugh John helped Mr. Frank fix his stable, where the cow had kicked a hole through the old wood in one wall and then panicked and tore the door off its sagging hinges. Maybe the cow hurt its leg in the hole; when it was caught later, one leg indeed had a wound, which Mr. Frank bound up with a rag.

Like it did a lot of older people, the Depression hit the Franks hard. As banks and the stock market crashed, savings and investments disappeared. To make matters worse, the Franks were in poor health and had no income apart from sell-ing some eggs and a little butter from their only cow. They would need to keep next year's calf rather than sell it for the small amount of cash it would bring—if the cow didn't die from the wound to its leg first. Then there would be no calf to become a replacement milker, and no butter to sell.

The Johnstones were their next-door neighbors on the other side. As the area blacksmith in a time before horses were replaced with tractors, Mr. Johnstone kept busy crafting and replacing horseshoes. In the winter he cut blocks of ice from the Red River to sell during summer's heat. We often had a stretch of 100-degree weather in July or August in southern Manitoba. The Johnstones were also the best customers for local fishermen. With several brood sows and fifty or so silver foxes to feed, they took all the dogfish, suckers, and other rough fish the fishermen couldn't sell anywhere else.

Like good neighbors, the Johnstones kept their eye on the Franks. When hog butchering time came around in the fall, Mrs. Johnstone took a package of souse and some chops to Mrs. Frank. During the winter, when their smoked hams and bacon were ready, Mrs. Johnstone would make another delivery. And through the warm weather, her husband kept the Frank's small icebox supplied.

Yet for the Johnstones, being a caring neighbor included something else, maintaining a sense of propriety and balance, key ingredients of humility and integrity. Mrs. Johnstone would accept a half-dozen eggs for the bacon and ham, and when Mrs. Frank pushed more at her, would say, "No, we take all your buttermilk for the brood sows. If it weren't for your buttermilk they wouldn't do nearly as well, and they wouldn't have so many healthy shoats."

When Mr. Johnstone delivered the ice, he would pick up the buttermilk and tell Mr. Frank, "I owe you another month's ice, Mr. Frank. Or would you like some more bacon?" The ice plus the ham and bacon and chops and souse were worth many times more than the buttermilk and a few eggs. So was Mr. Johnstone not telling the truth? Or was he instead keeping the commandment of God to love his neighbor?

The Johnstones could put any price they wanted on their deliveries—if we insist they must. The only thing they would insist on was keeping the dignity of a poor, elderly couple.

Mr. Johnstone couldn't help the Franks when their cow broke out of the barn. So he called my brother. Hugh John took some boards and a pocket full of nails from our shop and spent the morning patching the hole and reseating the hinges in the door. When he finished, Mrs. Frank asked if he would eat a bowl of tapioca.

Hugh sat at their worn kitchen table and choked down a couple spoons of water-blown tapioca. Mrs. Frank excused herself for a moment and stepped into the front room for her shawl. In desperation, Hugh dumped the rest of the bowl of pudding in his overall pocket, just before Mrs. Frank came back.

"You finished it already," she exclaimed. "You really must be hungry. Here, have another bowl!" Her pleasure glowed in her lined face, and he hadn't the heart to refuse.

"Just a little, thanks." He took up the spoon, and when Mrs. Frank sat down at the table opposite him, he swallowed the first spoonful. It almost came back. She smiled warmly. He swallowed another. "I can do this," he thought.

When he finished the bowl and excused himself to go home, the Franks were pleased he'd enjoyed the tapioca. "You've earned it," Mr. Frank said as he shook Hugh's hand. "Come again and have some more."

On the way out behind the house where the Franks

couldn't see him, Hugh emptied his pocket and rinsed it off under the pump. With a little humility and gritty determination, he had acknowledged the generous heart of his neighbors. And in caring enough to eat their meager offering, he preserved their dignity as hosts.

Eating has rich significance in the Bible, for good or ill. Eve shared some forbidden fruit with Adam and together they lost their innocence and their fellowship with God.[2] Much later in history, Daniel and his companions chose a vegetarian diet and plain water rather than eat of King Nebuchadnezzar's table, and found God's favor in insight and wisdom.[3]

In Jewish homes today, a seder—both meal and religious observance—commemorates Passover and the deliverance of Israel from slavery in Egypt by the grace of God.[4] Each family celebrates in its own home, yet as part of "the whole congregation of Israel."[5]

The meal is full of symbolism. Matzoth, unleavened bread, reminds them of the urgency [6] of the last meal in their homes in Egypt, when they had no time to let the bread rise. *Zeroa*, a roasted lamb shank, recalls to them the shared Paschal lamb, its blood painted on the doorposts and lintel to protect the home from the plague of death the Lord brought upon Egypt.[7] *Maror* or bitter herbs, often horseradish or romaine lettuce in today's seder, reminds the eater of the harshness of slavery, and a bowl of salt water, in which parsley is dipped, recalls the tears of the oppressed. *Haroseth*, a mix of chopped apples, nuts, wine, and spices, becomes a symbol of the mortar used by the slaves, overlaid by the sweetness of their redemption.

Four cups of wine speak of four different expressions of redemption. The Haggadah is recited; hymns and poems tell of their deliverance "by God alone." The seder is designed to pass on the story of God's salvation to the next generation, beginning with the first question of the youngest child, "Why is this night different from all other nights?"

For the celebrants, the seder becomes a powerful means to reinforce their understanding of the reality of God.

With similar intensity of meaning, this was the meal Jesus shared with his disciples the night before his arrest and execution. His actions and words at his last supper rise out of the Passover and its place in Jewish life. Jesus reached into the *What Is* of God, that larger reality we find so hard to grasp, and identified his body with the unleavened bread of the Passover, his blood with that of the Paschal lamb.

Jesus told his followers they could "eat" and "drink" the presence of God. As Jesus "absorbed" the reality of God into his being, we can, too: "Take, eat; this is my body. . . . Drink . . . this is my blood."[8]

That is, if we too are willing to be as he was, to be one with God in his purpose for our world, to be challenged, renovated, and guided by his presence, his Spirit becoming our spirit, anointing our heads, hearts, and hands. At his last meal with his friends, he even washed their feet in another transforming act,[9] anointing them completely to serve others as he had been anointed to serve them.

In spite of all the enemies that surround us, no matter the stresses that seem so unconquerable, the presence of God can and will overflow our lives with his grace. And in the same mysterious way, like Jesus, we can become bread and blood for others.

The knitting together of two lives in marriage gives us a snapshot of the process.[10] When two people commit themselves to the smelting furnace of marriage, unusual things begin to happen. Norma and I didn't have any idea or clue of what lay ahead when we decided we couldn't live apart any longer.

We loved each other with suitable passion, shared some interests, and even liked each other enough to want to spend lots of time together. Maybe that's all you can expect for a start. But what a risk to take, when you know so little of what lies ahead.

The commitment we made to each other was surrounded on all sides by the enemies we brought with us, enemies we dared not admit we harbored. "What's in this relationship for me?" "Will she take more from me than I can give?" "Can I really be responsible for a life other than my own?" It's one thing to fall in love, quite another to move into a relationship that calls for self-giving day after day, year after year.

Of such tentative commitments is faith expressed. And God pours out his grace in abundant anointing.

Couples who have survived years of married life successfully know how much they have changed and have been changed over the years. The grace of God shines on the hesitant steps of faith young couples take together, the willing-to-grow steps each one takes as events come along—such as the arrival of a baby. Few events can match having a child to shake up and rearrange a marriage.

When our first baby was born, we knew less than zip about infant care. It was the era when new mothers faced long hospital stays and debilitating bed rest, while fathers were exiled to distant orbit from birthing rooms. Not even God the Father could get past an ob-gyn nurse then to see his son being born.

Norma discovered Benjamin Spock when our first born, Jim, was about six months old, and she used up three copies of Spock's *Common Sense Book of Baby and Childcare* on our four children. It was an open window of advice in an otherwise closed room, but not even Spock could have helped us in our first crisis, about two weeks after Jim was born.

I believe our pediatrician would have preferred to use stone tablets to inscribe his prescriptions. The man had an attitude as haughty and forbidding as it was distant; he seems to have thought God was created in his image. When Norma took baby Jim on his first visit, the pediatrician insisted Norma give up breast-feeding and turn to infant formula instead. Back then some authorities believed formula feeding to be more controllable than the old-fashioned nourishment, and more acceptable in public.

Then he declared the baby's navel was an "outie" and needed to be bound. So he wrapped a swath of wide adhesive tape almost completely around his body and wee Jim began to cry.

He cried all afternoon. When I got home from work, Norma was frantic. She had fed him some formula—he threw it up; he couldn't keep anything down.

As the evening wore on, his wails became more forsaken and strident. Norma rocked Jim in his carriage, but he would curl his little body and shriek in anguish. She was still weakened from seven days in bed, and really needed a friend with some fresh legs.

I learned to dance a baby that long, long night. We discovered if Jim was held firmly against my stomach and rocked in a generous, weaving dance, his little body could relax a little, his cries softening to sobs and whimpers.

The first time his crying eased, we thought he might go to sleep. Norma took him gently and laid him in his crib. But as soon as she let go of his body, he arched his back and screamed. She looked at me with tears running down her face.

"This is enough." She picked Jim up again and held him out to me, "I'm calling the doctor." But all she got was an answering service, and since it was already so late she was to call back in the morning.

I danced some more; held him tight; swaddled him with my arms, hand beneath his head. He would not cry quite as fiercely, his little body would not squirm and twist quite so desperately.

I don't know how we lasted. He was so tiny, so much in agony, so helpless, and utterly dependent. We were so helpless and utterly dependent on a doctor we couldn't reach.

That long night I learned a lot about the young woman I had married. She was totally focused on the tiny child she walked, singing gently to his sobs. When she tired, I would dance him some more—but she was there, watching, thinking, and planning. By the time the sun began to lighten the sky, she had determined to call another pediatrician, father of a close friend. He had retired just before Jim was born.

Dr. Day was about to have breakfast, and how could he help? Norma told him of little Jim's ceaseless crying, how he twisted in pain. She told him about the bandage.

"What bandage?"

"Around his middle."

- "Elasticized?"

"No, just adhesive tape. Over his navel. It bulges."

"Take it off. Right now. Grab it at one end and pull it off in one steady pull."

I'd never before noticed the swift concentration of a

mother fighting for her child. Norma picked at the end of the tape until she could get a firm grip—then pulled it quickly across the little belly.

"I've killed him!" she whispered. The baby's head rolled limply to one side, the crying silenced as if switched off.

"No, he's still breathing. His lips are sucking. He's asleep!"

Wee Jim slept on for seven hours. Then he drank ravenously, burped mightily, and slept again. His cup overflowed. Although we did not realize it then, Norma and I had drawn upon the abundant anointing of God.

We had been surrounded by enemies that long night. The arrogant pediatrician who started it all was only one of many. There was our fathomless inexperience, one of the worst enemies we all carry with us, betraying us at every turn. There was our fear of the unknown. How dare we be parents to this little thing, he so dependent, and we so ignorant. Another enemy, our growing anger—aimed at what? Add the tension and strength-sapping fatigue that could have turned us against one another, or worse, against the baby.

Yet God was doing something for us, to us. In the midst of the baby's pain and our confused anxiety, God was anointing us with the oil of experience—together, the oil of new responsibility—together; the oil of love for this wondrous gift so dependent on our care—together. We made a lot of mistakes on this first child, but loving him was not one of them. Jim is a fine man now, a skilled physician and loving father.

In the midst of our enemies that night, God spread a table to nourish us. Even more, he poured out his anointing grace in such abundance that we have never been the same since. We grew into caring parents in new ways, new depths that night. Like so many parents have done, before us and since, we discovered how to stay a scant step ahead of disaster most of the time.

But even when we can't avoid disaster, even in the worst of times, the grace of God is there.

*I don't want our generation to worsen the world.
I hope we can make it better for the next
generation. First, I want my kids to turn
out well, I want to be a parent like my
Mom and Dad. Then I really hope that I can
find a useful occupation and that my life turns out
at least roughly the way God intended it to be.*

—Megan

*Children are the living message we send
to a time we will not see.*

—John W. Whitehead

ELEVEN

Surely Goodness and Mercy Shall Follow Me All the Days of My Life . . .

onday I called the 800-number for the credit card department at our bank. There was an $8.57 charge on our bill we weren't sure about. Not a good way to start the week. We rarely use plastic unless we get in a bind, like the time I filled up on gas before I checked my wallet. No cash. The card saved the situation.

Our bank started out as a local institution, but along the way it was swallowed by a regional shark swimming in the financial waters. A few years later a bigger shark made a meal of the regional bank, and we are the beneficiaries, supposedly. Now when we go into a branch there are six tellers to serve customers where there used to be 12. Makes for the joy of waiting in line.

That Monday an automated voice answered my call. I listened to the "menu" and punched number four to get a real voice. I was put on hold, of course, complete with elevator music and the recorded assurance every minute or so, "We are sorry there is no one available to take your call at this time. We value your business and as soon as possible someone will be with you." I think there were four different versions of this endearing message, just in case I got bored and hung up. But it didn't work. I wasn't bored, I was frustrated and annoyed.

Automated public relations will never replace human beings, and somebody in the automated ideas department ought to learn that truth by being put on hold at least twice a day.

Finally a real voice answered, and she explained what I needed to know. Before she hung up, I asked how many difficult customers she had to deal with every day. And how did she keep her cool?

When the surprise level settled in her voice, I could hear a smile. She was really a very nice person, and had a nasty job to do. "I try not to let the stress get to me," she said. "In the evening I like to do a little gardening or go for a walk to unwind. But some days are worse than others."

How many calls does she get to process every day? A lot more than she used to; now she's expected to handle well over a hundred calls each day. No wonder I was dangled on hold for so long, gnawing on my irritations.

A few enlightened corporations have begun to understand that the mental and physical well-being of their employees is good for the long-term "bottom line." But a few is not enough, and that means most of us will have to live with the pressure. So we can either let anger double our frustration and stress, or we can let God ease the load with his goodness and mercy.

Some biblical scholars think the writer of Psalm 23 pic-
tured here the assistants or attendants who followed a digni-
tary to do his bidding, and named them Goodness and Mercy.
Others see two sheep dogs helping the Shepherd, the helpers
named for the characteristics of the work they do for the
sheep.

But can "goodness" and "mercy" help in a hard-nosed business environment? It's hard to hear the Shepherd's sheep dogs
when the wolves are snapping at our heels. How can we walk
in faith when we're being pushed and prodded by an unfriend-
ly situation on the job?

I believe there are many, many people who have discovered the help of God in the hard places of life. They will insist
goodness and mercy have reached through from the Shepherd
and made it possible to survive. For them, life-transforming
surprises begin at the point of contact between "hard-nosed
reality" and the reality of God.

Make no mistake, every difficult situation is stressful, and
stress can be deadly. A little stress is good for us; a lot of
unmanaged stress is not.¹ Cumulative stress can make our lives
miserable, even kill us. So if we are created in the image, in
the likeness of God, why can such an enemy as stress get at us?

Our grasp of reality knows that bad things happen to us all.
We don't need to be paranoid to know there are nasty, evil,
good-threatening processes going on in the world. But then
again, if we're supposed to learn and grow in faith, then fac-
ing and going through the bad is as necessary for us as learning to walk. So the idea is not just how to manage or control
our stresses, but how to cooperate with God in using them to
move us to the next stage in our development in his reality.
Each successful experience makes way for another, no matter
how small the success may be.

John, our second son, discovered one way to handle his stress and learn from it when he was still a child. When his energy levels started to get him in trouble inside, we would tell him, "John, go out and run around the house." He was a cheerful boy and understood the command as a generic statement, meaning, "Find a better way to use your excess energy than bouncing off the walls."

Sometimes he'd push his scooter down the block and visit a friend, other times he did actually go out and run a few laps. Always he returned with a new interest in mind, a new project to occupy his energies. He was ready to move on.

It became a part of his life. Along the way, John learned to balance the intensity of his research in computer science with high-energy exercise—swimming, running, long walks. He found it not only eases the tension, but frees his mind to find creative answers to the problems he's working on. He took steps to "listen" to the *What Is*. Goodness and mercy followed.

If we don't pay attention to where we are in relation to the *What Is* of God, we won't learn to handle our stress in the right way. Much of the advice we get on stress tends to treat the symptoms rather than the cause: our inability to handle the conflict between the everyday world around us and the realm God is creating for us. He offers us disciplines of change as part of *What Is*, and he expects us to make them a living part of our lives and not something tacked on to handle stress, because something tacked on isn't apt to last. And it will take a lifelong commitment to his way, since the kind of disciplines we need call for lifelong attention to how *What Is* works.

If you've tried to lose weight or quit smoking, you may

have found you need more help than you can muster in your-self. But God won't turn off a habit switch any more than he will lower our cholesterol levels for us; we must first decide to focus on his reality, seek out his rightness in our lives, and arm ourselves with his grace.[2] Then we'll make some discoveries about our capabilities and his strength.

From all we know of God, he won't step in to change our natures if we let anger dominate our driving, if we cheat on our spouses, or call in sick when we're heading for the beach. But he can and will encourage our desire to change and move toward his image. And he will provide us the strength we need to take the appropriate actions.[3] When we take a step of faith toward his integrity, we will find his grace is there to help; always has been and always will be there. As we eat of God's table, his goodness and mercy will follow, all the days of our lives.

We learned some more about his discipline of patience when we tried to find a place to live we could afford. As the two years we spent getting reacquainted with Nova Scotia wound down to the final months, we wondered where we would stay on our return to the Shenandoah Valley.

Just before Christmas I called the Schaefers, near where we had lived before. After I explained who was calling and why, I asked Elaine if she knew of a place to rent in the area.

Yes, she did know. Only the night before she and John had decided to rent their old farmhouse for a few years, so they could live with John's aging parents and take care of them. The Lord our Shepherd was preparing a place for us.[4] Two months later we drove a Ryder truck full of our stuff into the driveway at Schaefers and began to unload.

I was working on *The Grace Connection*[5] at the time. We knew we'd need to find our own place soon, so whenever we had a few minutes, we would look at house listings in the paper and call realtors. But we had a problem: everything we looked at had something wrong with it. Too far away. Too big. Too expensive. No trees. In town. Didn't feel like the right place for us.

When our older daughter, Debby, expressed concern for our future, Norma told her, "The Lord does have a home for us, we just haven't found it yet. But we'll know it when we see it."

Then when daughter Cathy needed to find a new situation, the man who owned the small farm across the road from our rented home knocked on the door. "Want to take over my place?" Ron Webb asked. Ron had an old farmhouse fixer-upper we could afford if Cathy bought the land and farm buildings around us so she could start her horse business.

For us all, finding a home has been an unmistakable provision of the Shepherd's goodness and mercy, another evidence of the *What Is* of God at work.

As I pointed out earlier, researchers have come up with many ways to help reduce stress. Most libraries carry books on stress reduction practices. Regular exercise, as vigorous as your doctor will agree to, is a good one. Developing control of your brain wave activity is another, by something like self-hypnosis (autogenics) or by imagining you are in your favorite peaceful spot (theater of the mind, some call it). Transcendental Meditation has been proven to reduce hypertension in clinical trials. All these techniques require training, and can be helpful.

One of the simplest ways to reduce stress is to learn how to relax. Sit comfortably. Start with toes and fingers, then move up through arms and legs to the whole body, consciously encouraging each group of muscles to relax. Take slow, deep breaths. Help your mind stop whirling by thinking only of the air being breathed in and out of your nose. After a few minutes of this, most of us can come down to a more relaxed, less stressed-out state.

Yet, when we're intensely worried about something, it takes more self-control than most of us can muster to come down from an adrenaline high. What we need is a route of faith, a routine we can follow that will allow God to help us not only with our stress but with our growth in his reality.

Each of us has our own situation to live through with the grace of God. If it will help, here are some pieces from the Bible that have taught me much about how to cooperate with the Lord Shepherd. The segments lend themselves to a sequence of steps I wish I'd followed faithfully every time the alligators crowded around.

1. *Commit your way to the Lord; trust in him, and he will act.*[6] Put who you are and your circumstances in God's hands. The best form of prayer and meditation is to commit yourself to God's presence and purpose as you think through your situation, trying to find a plan or two that might bring resolution to your life. If you're in a complicated, demanding situation, try not to despair. Trust God to begin to open a way for you. Keep praying, even if you don't feel like it.

2. Find someone to confide in, someone who can help with advice, someone with integrity. Too often I forgot this until later, plunging ahead on my own; not a good idea. Jesus told his listeners, *If two of you agree on earth about anything you ask, it will be done for you by my Father in heaven. For where two*

or three are gathered in my name, I am there among them.[7] Pray some more, even if it's in the back of your mind, on the edge of your spirit.

3. Decide on a step or steps to take as a first move. Remember, God won't push but he will steer. You don't have to know what's next for your life; even a small step will give you the opportunity to see where God might want you to go. *Trust in the Lord with all your heart, and do not rely on your own insight. In all your ways acknowledge him, and he will make straight your paths.*[8]

4. *We know that all things work together for good for those who love God.*[9] Check that your action won't hurt someone else. This is a messy one, sometimes whatever you do seems bound to hurt someone you care for; be patient and watch how God works things out. The late Dr. Hans Selye, one of the leaders in stress research, reinterpreted the commandment "Love your neighbor as you love yourself." Selye wanted to put a practical turn to it, so he chose to live by the philosophy "Earn your neighbor's love."[10]

5. Now, having committed your way to the Shepherd and set things in motion, try to relax. Easier said than done, but unless you've missed a turn somewhere, the "goodness and mercy of God" will follow the steps of faith you've taken. Then, in the midst of your enemies, you will discover the peace of God's way—*those who wait for the Lord shall renew their strength, they shall mount up with wings like eagles, they shall run and not be weary, they shall walk and not faint.*[11]

All of us must discover our own responses to the situations we get into. God will shape the disciplines of change we need in order to "work out our own salvation."[12] But be prepared to go through yet another dilemma in your life, and learn another discipline of faith. Learning the height and depth and strength of the grace of God is a lifelong cycle of such experiences. We hit a wall of circumstance that we try to climb over on our own, then rediscover our need for something more than we've got in ourselves, and drag faith out of wherever we've hidden it and start to look for God's help.

Then once again we find that he has been waiting to help us grow a little more into his image. Once again, in another of life's ever-changing situations, we experience his grace. Once more we know why the psalmist wrote, "Surely goodness and mercy shall follow me all the days of my life."

Back in the first century, Paul didn't have to worry much about pressure on the job. He made and repaired tents for a living; it gave him flexible hours and he could set up shop anywhere. Herdsmen used tents on summer pasture in the high country and there was a steady market among shopkeepers for awnings.

Paul never spoke of his problems making tents. He was much more concerned about the faith-life of the people he met and brought to the *What Is* of God, and it's in this work that he talked of his greatest disappointments and frustrations.[13] He had no illusions about human nature and its need for all the help God can give us against our spiritual enemies.

When Paul talked of this help, he used word pictures all his readers could understand. Roman soldiers were everywhere, keeping the peace and defending the empire. Like police today, they carried deadly weapons and wore protective body armor.

Paul insists the person who walks by faith can call on God

to provide all the protection needed against the forces of evil, within and without. "Take up the whole armor of God," Paul directs.[14] Take up all of it, so that even on the worst day of our lives, we can stand firm in the reality of God, integrity intact.

Paul tells us to "fasten the belt of truth around your waist," then add "put on the breastplate of righteousness." Like a Kevlar vest, right living under the direction of the Lord Shepherd lets us walk with confidence through assaults by what Paul describes as the "powers of this present darkness," in all the many combinations of inner arrogance and outer temptation.

A genuine walk of faith is one of reconciliation, a gospel we become eager to share. Understanding the gospel of truth and justice puts shoes on our feet to make peace wherever we go. Faith in God's reality becomes a shield to use in every circumstance against "the flaming arrows of the evil one."

Therefore, Paul's argument goes, no matter what today throws at us, we have a sure defense. Whatever we are becoming, whatever we know ourselves to be in Christ is covered with the "helmet of salvation," in all that God has done to make our new life possible.

This package Paul called salvation is an eternal provision—the forever Word of God—spoken into human history by his Spirit, our sword. It cuts through all the sophistry and spin doctoring, including the self-justifying arguments we come up with as we go our own way. The *What Is* of God cuts through and judges the thoughts and intentions of our hearts.[15]

And our final weapon is prayer, in all things at all times, including prayer for all who are with us in the resurrected body of Christ.[16] Since God is preparing a people to live out his nature, is it any wonder he provides all we'll ever need in order to do so by giving us all the power of his strength and the strength of his power?

Surely goodness and mercy shall follow me all the days of my life . . .

*I find e-mail and telephones to be an inadequate
substitution for a person's actual presence.
For me, the only interesting things in life are
the people I've met. . . . Resources don't
make a country rich, people do. My greatest
hope is to be surrounded by people I love,
and to be able to relate to others with integrity.*

—Austin

*[We ignore] what an enormous shock the new
[technology] . . . may be. . . . It's time to stop
pretending that our demands for greater
knowledge have no downside. It's time we
faced the fact that this new era, for all the
miracles it has wrought, disrupts age-old
cultural and even biological patterns.*

—Larry Letich

TWELVE

And I Shall Dwell in the House of the Lord My Whole Life Long.

I loved hockey, it was the game most kids played all winter in Manitoba, but football was my first experience in serious teamwork. When I was 13, my father took me to see the Winnipeg Blue Bombers play in the Canadian Football League, and I was hooked. So in Grade 11 at Kelvin High School, when Coach Les Lear allowed me to suit up, I was his most eager recruit. He warned me I'd see game action only if I beefed up a little; I think the water boy was bigger than me. I never did beef up enough, so I got to be hammered on by the real players in practice and gained a few pounds of bruises.

I missed a season with bad tonsils. The year after, I tried out for the University of Manitoba team; I was 17, had put on a few pounds, and the coach figured I might make a second string tight end. We played a college in North Dakota and a couple exhibition games against teams in the CFL. This was 1943 and by then the only civilian football players left in town were men who had ripped up knees or held essential jobs in wartime industries—or kids like me.

As the saying goes, "Fools rush in where angels fear to tread." I should've quit while I was ahead. We played a night game against the Blue Bombers, the best team in the conference. That night I tackled CFL star running back Fritz Hanson in the open field, and the hook just bit in a little deeper.

Next fall on a new team our quarterback was a tough little American who wore soda-bottle-bottom glasses in rubber frames. He was fast, a good passer, and pulled together an odd bunch of young players and veterans. I remember him saying again and again, "You do your job so I can do mine." It sounds trite now, but it stuck with me then.

First game, I had the job of blocking out Tiny Lucid, an aging defensive lineman with the Blue Bombers. He was big, and despite his aching bones, could move me out of the way most plays. I heard it sharply in the huddle, "Do your job Fairfield, so I can do mine." Next play came my way, I wrapped my arms around Tiny when the ref wasn't looking. On another play I fell down around Lucid's boots and tripped him; this time the ref saw me. Ten yard penalty, my fault big time.

What's a tight end do when he's outweighed by 60 some pounds? Complain? I heaved high so he had to go over me. Hit low and he fell on me. Not a good idea. Got in Lucid's face till we both got confused. Sometimes it worked, most times I just slowed him up a little. It was a frustrating experience in humility—but blocking him out was my job.

Most of us find out the hard way that it isn't easy doing what we're asked to do in life. Especially when others depend on us to do it right.

~

As we get to the last section of Psalm 23, the writer changes metaphors, from being a sheep of the Shepherd to being a guest at the Lord's table, invited to spend the rest of his days in the Lord's house. He goes through a process of change, from sheeplike ignorance of his place in the *What Is* of God to a mature recognition of his need for discipline and direction as one of God's team-people. It amounts to the choice of where he is going to live out his life, in the house of the Lord, or in one of his own making.

For the psalmist, living in the house of God begins in humility, grows in discipline, and matures as an anointed guest of the Lord. It's a matter of who we are, where we are with our lives, and why. As I understand it, the "house of the Lord" is his reality, his realm, the *What Is* of God. All that God has accomplished since the creation of the universe takes on meaning in what he is doing in the people of faith who have submitted their lives to him, no matter where that faith is found.[1]

There are many kinds of people in the house of the Lord. In his mansion there are rooms for all. How they describe their faith may sound different from the way we do, but the God whose grace they know and we know is One. Our job is not to tell him who he can love and accept; ours is to walk with him humbly where we are found, and be agents of his mercy and justice.

Jesus painted parable-pictures of the *What Is* of his Father. Again and again he began a story with "The kingdom of God is like . . ." and went on to try to open our eyes to its reality. Over the centuries since then, an imperfect image of *What Is* has emerged—blurry snapshots of the Lord's house—as his people have congregated to help each other do their "job" in response to the guidance of the Shepherd.

⁓

Paul discovered something in his transformation: He had become a "member of a body." He was not just one of the people of God but more—a part of a living entity, the "body of Christ," a picture-parable of fingers and feet, eyes and ears, lesser parts and greater parts, all working together in faith to be the *What Is* of God in the world.[2]

It became for Paul the centerpiece of his mission: in Christ's "body" God is creating a way to express his integrity to the nations of the world.[3] The communion meal Christians eat together, like the meal the couple on the way to Emmaus shared with the stranger, affirms that understanding. It represents the reality of God in the world through his people.

In another attempt to explain our interdependence rather than our independence, Jesus used a different picture: "I am the vine and you are the branches." He expected that as his people became one with him they would fulfill the will of God for their lives. In effect, Jesus expected them to become part of his "replacement body," greater than his alone.[4]

Jesus astounded the crowd who followed him when he said, "Those who eat my flesh and drink my blood abide in me, and I in them."[5] They failed to grasp the significance of becoming part of his "kingdom" reality. When they heard Jesus speak of these things, many of his followers turned their backs on him. "This sort of talk is hard to endure! How can anyone take it seriously?"[6] When all but a few left him, Jesus faced his trial and death alone, with only his trust in the grace of God. Yet it was enough.

Even though the few were frightened at his capture and watched from a distance at his execution, Jesus was convinced that, with the grace of God at work in them, the kingdom would move out into the world and succeed in its mission. He knew the future would be assured; it took only a few to make a start—even a few as frightened as Peter, who denied him more than once.

Now through their faith and faithfulness,[7] we can come alive as Jesus is alive, and his "body" is with us in each other.

We don't get to "live in the house of the Lord" because we never make a mistake. None of us would ever make it. We'd be left in our guilt, like Peter, wondering what went wrong with who we thought we were. On the night Jesus was captured and sentenced to death, Peter denied he even knew Jesus.[8] That is when Peter found out how fragile faith can be— and how strong the forgiving grace of the Lord Shepherd.

Peter blew it again some years later when he went up to Antioch to visit the people of The Way there. They were a mixed bag—Jewish believers as well as uncircumcised ex-pagans who were being called Christians for the first time.[9] But Peter got along well with them, even broke bread with them in memory of Jesus, until some of his cohorts from Jerusalem showed up. Then he withdrew and ate only with the "circumcision group." It became another serious denial that Paul had to challenge and make right.[10]

But Peter survived his failures. Each experience became an opportunity to find out more about himself, and more about the renewing forgiveness of God. Jesus, like the prophets before him,[11] made it clear that forgiveness is one of the gifts grace brings to us. We need forgiveness, repeatedly, and we will receive it if we're humble enough to seek it.[12] Then our transformation into a new creation can continue.

Again and again Jesus urges all who will listen to turn around, turn away from the false ideas we have of *What Is* and

see that the kingdom of God is "at hand." The reality that has
the power to forgive and transform surrounds us, is within the
reach of even the smallest faith, and because the "house of the
Lord" is our proper home, it brings new life in his grace.

In the *What Is* of God we are forgiven and renewed by the
presence and wholeness of his Spirit.[13]

Consider the experience of Tamar, grieving wife and childless widow. She had been given in marriage to the prince of
the tribe of Judah, forefather of the Jews. Tamar's husband Er
was to inherit the leadership and a double share of Judah's
wealth. His son, Tamar's son, would receive a similar inheri-
tance, but Er died childless and Tamar's future collapsed. Her
story is found in chapter 38 of the book of Genesis.

The law decreed that the dead man's oldest brother should
take over his wife so that she would bear a son. Judah demanded his second son, Onan, fulfill this obligation, to "raise up
offspring for your brother." But Onan had his own children
and his own hopes to inherit in mind, so he refused to impreg-
nate Tamar. Soon after, he was dead.

Bearing a grandson to Judah was vitally important to
Tamar. In effect she was the crown princess of her tribe and
her parents expected much of this marriage. But a childless
widow faced a dim future indeed. So when Judah promised her
that his third son, Shelah, would take her husband's place in
a year or so when he matured, she counted on his word.

Yet Judah feared Tamar's effect on men; two of his sons
who knew her had died. Was he to lose his third son as well?
So although he had promised Shelah to her, he sent Tamar
back to her father's house and ignored his covenant.

Then Judah's own wife died. After a period of mourning,

Judah planned a trip to his sheep-shearing camp. When Tamar heard about it, she put off her widow's garments and dressed herself as a prostitute. She knew that Shelah had matured, yet had not been given to her in marriage, so she sat down on the road to the sheep camp and waited for Judah.

When Judah saw her, he thought she was a prostitute because she had covered her face; he did not recognize Tamar. He asked if he could lie with her. She said, "What will you give me, that you may come in to me?" He promised a kid from his goats. Tamar asked for a pledge from him until he sent the kid. Judah asked what she would take as a pledge. She replied, "Your signet seal and its neck-cord, and the staff you carry."

Judah gave these to her and had intercourse with Tamar, then went on to his camp. She went back to her father's home so that when Judah sent a friend with the goat-kid to recover his pledge, there was no prostitute to be found.

Three months later Judah was told, "Your daughter-in-law Tamar has played the whore and she is pregnant as a result." Judah pronounced sentence, "Bring her out, and let her be burned to death." As she was taken from her father's home, Tamar sent word to her father-in-law, "It was the owner of these who made me pregnant." She pointed out, "Please take note whose these are, the signet seal with its neck-cord, and the staff."

The shock for Judah cleared his vision, and he saw himself in the light of *What Is*. He stopped the execution of Tamar, and publicly cleared her name. "She is more right than I, since I did not give her to my son Shelah."

In this convoluted story it's hard to discern the right from the muddy and the wrong from expediency. Nevertheless, without the fierce determination of Tamar to take her place in the "house of the Lord," there would have been no Jesus. In Matthew's Gospel, the lineage of Jesus goes back to Perez, the oldest of the twins Tamar bore to Judah.

There is much in the world that is not wholesome or consistent, loving or forgiving. Arrogance and insolence, malice and scorn, greed and envy infect our world like the plague, giving evidence of the small, self-centered character that falls short of the image of God.

This small self misses the mark on everything, and we miss the integrity of God that is our hope.

Nevertheless, God calls us out of the small into a larger self, freeing us to live in his nature and purpose. He gives us the privilege of doing something with our lives, not to "earn" merit but to exercise the grace he can pour through our lives to overflowing. We are not "saved" for nothing; salvation from sin, from the enemies we carry with us, is but a bare deliverance. We are to grow into the image of God as we create his community here on earth.

We are never out of the reach of God. If our own problems and stresses were the only ones we had to worry about, life might seem a lot simpler.

But we are woven into a fabric of other lives, a family, a community, a workplace. This richly textured fabric is the reality of God, the *What Is* of creation. Through these human connections we experience the dynamics that can shape us more and more into the image of God.

In the house of the Lord, people of faith work together to reinforce integrity wherever it appears, strengthen love as a forgiving and cleansing power, intensify kindness and mercy, uphold justice—particularly for the poor and dispossessed—

and encourage faith and trust in God and his reality. The house of the Lord becomes a power of reconciliation and a refuge of peace.

Whenever we share the abundance of his grace with others, we move on from life in a spiritual kindergarten to life on another level, in the Lord's house, his community. Paul reminds us of the living evidence of God's community: "Whatever is true, whatever is honorable, whatever is just, whatever is pure, whatever is pleasing, whatever is commendable, if there is any excellence and if there is anything worthy of praise, think about these things."

Then Paul adds, "Keep on doing the things that you have learned and received and heard and seen in me, and the God of peace will be with you."[14]

In a walk of faith we won't sidestep stress. Stress is a fact of life and we are bound to experience devastating amounts of it, sooner or later. But stress—like humiliation—need not destroy us *if we use it as an opportunity to find the way* through to a better, larger life on the other side, for the rest of our days, our whole life long. As we survive our stresses and conflicts with the grace of God, we are being trained to act and think as he does, to love and care for others as he does. We are called to bring his reality into being in the midst of a hostile, deadly atmosphere.[15]

Whenever we choose to love and forgive, to live in kindness and honesty, to act justly and generously, then stressful situations must yield their damaging power. Sooner or later, something creative must happen.

When our lives are established on the reality of the Lord our Shepherd, then, no matter the conditions, they must begin to change for something better, and even death must lose its sting.[16]

We don't have to go back to some point in the past in order for our lives to be restructured, instead we go on from where we are now. Each day as we live it, we will make choices. If we choose the Lord-Shepherd—*I AM WHAT I AM*—we will find authentic fulfillment in the reality of God. As we turn away from all that is not *I AM*, we cut off its power to harm us. We move on in the great adventure of being shaped in the integrity of God.

It doesn't take much faith to choose *I AM WHAT I AM*, only the kind of faith a child has in the worthiness of life, the faith we have whenever we think, "There is a better way to live than I am living now." And having made the choice to follow the Lord-Shepherd, we will find that the ability and power to change our lives is within us, closer than we ever imagined. His spirit will lift our spirits, setting us free to grow in his disciplines. Stresses and circumstances will become stepping-stones of experience in the grace of God.

And I shall dwell in the house of the Lord my whole life long.

Study Guide
and References

A personal study of the Bible can make a profound difference in anyone's life, especially when shared with others. The
Spirit of God has more to say to us through others as we work
together in the body of Christ. Here is a double study: of
Psalm 23 and its riches, plus a consideration of stress from a
biblical perspective. To help stimulate discussion, this guide
provides several starter questions for each chapter. In addi-
tion, references keyed to note numbers in the text give verifi-
cation and opportunity for further research.

Study group leaders: There is more to human nature than
what we see and sense. It is difficult for us to tell each other
exactly how God is working in our lives, particularly as we go
through periods of anxiety and confusion. We face two problems. One is in understanding ourselves and how the Spirit of
Jesus is reaching us. The other is finding the right words to
talk about this ongoing experience accurately. Encourage the
members of your group to explore this area of their lives as the
primary goal of your work together.

Your local library can provide many more books and arti-

cles on stress than you will want to read. If your group express-
es interest, make a list of the more up-to-date titles and invite
members to select one to read, and ask one member to sum up
a book briefly at each meeting. What does the author say
about stress? What recommendations are made? Does the
writer allow room for God?

Aims: To help each other develop a new understanding of
the biblical "reality of God" as over against lesser ideas of reality. Encourage use of a study-diary. As you move into later
chapters, explore the *What Is* of God, the reality of his realm,
in his continuing creation of the body of Christ. Invite
insights relative to God's purpose for the church at the beginning and at the end of chapter 5, and as you come to the end
of the book.

1. The Lord Is My Shepherd . . . Define for yourself good
stress and bad stress. In what ways have you experienced
stress? How do humility and humiliation relate in your life?
Do you think there is a relationship between biblical righteousness and personal integrity? How does integrity relate to
the I AM of God? What terms would you use to describe the
righteousness of God?

References: Hans Selye, M.D., *Health in Stress and Disease*.
Boston: Butterworth, 1976, p. 729. (1) Associated Press report
from Washington cited in the *Daily News Record*,
Harrisonburg, Virginia, March 7, 1995. (2) *In Sync*,
Winter/Spring 1995, Pamela Gilchrist, ed. Erie Insurance
Group, Erie, Pennsylvania. (3) Possibly the best introduction
to stress for the general reader is *The Stress of Life* by Hans
Selye, M.D., published by McGraw-Hill Book Company, New
York, 1976. (4) Hebrews 11:1, Romans 1:16-17. (5) Exodus

3:14. (6) Micah 6:8. (7) Genesis 3:1-13. (8) Romans 5:10-14; 1 Corinthians 15:45-49. (9) John 8:42-47. (10) John 8:51. (11) John 10:19-20. (12) John 8:53. (13) Galatians 5:22. (14) John 8:56-58. (15) 2 Corinthians 5:16-17; Romans 6:1-4.

2. I Shall Not Want . . . In what ways has culture shaped our understanding of wants and needs? Do you think living in an affluent country makes it harder or easier to walk with God? What are your reasons? Do you accept the idea that we are driven by our need for security? Which stress-reduction method appeals to you? Why? How can we be sure any action we take is ethical and appropriate?

References: Lauren Sill as told to Natalee Roth, *Together*, Spring 2000. (1) Matthew 6:31-34. (2) Isaiah 48:17; Psalm 31:3-5. (3) Matthew 19:16-22. (4) Matthew 19:23-24. (5) Matthew 6:24. (6) Matthew 6:26. (7) Matthew 6:33. (8) Luke 14:26. (9) John 3:1-7; Romans 6:1-5. (10) 2 Corinthians 5:16, 17.

3. He Makes Me Lie Down in Green Pastures . . . If you have had an experience of peace in the midst of turmoil, how have you explained it to yourself and to others? What did you learn from the event? If the Bible condenses human experience, how does it deal with fear? How has your life, until now, taught you to deal with your anxieties and stresses?

References: Jesus speaks to his disciples in John 10:3-5, paraphrased. (1) 1 Samuel 10:17-24; 16:1-13. (2) 1 Samuel 1:20. (3) 1 Samuel 1:27-28. (4) 1 Samuel 2:12-17, 22-24. (5) The story of Samuel's call is paraphrased from 1 Samuel 3:1-10. (6) 2 Timothy 2:13. (7) Proverbs 3:5-6. (8) Matthew

4:17. (9) Matthew 5:3. (10) Luke 17:20-21. (11) John 14:27. (12) Philippians 4:6-7.

4. He Leads Me Beside Still Waters; He Restores My Soul . . . What mirror have you found to show you who you are? What steps of faith will be necessary for your soul to be restored? Think of the people you know who have demonstrated to you the "likeness" of God. In what ways have you seen God in them?

References: Jeremiah 17:7-8. (1) Adapted from John 4:1-42, New American Bible, and New Revised Standard Version. (2) Genesis 1:26-27.

5. He Leads Me in Right Paths for His Name's Sake . . . What is it you hope people will remember when they hear your name? Select some words you feel best describe the right paths of the Lord Shepherd. If it is difficult to pin down moral and ethical standards, how can we know what is the way of integrity? How does Jesus sum up all standards and laws? Does this mean we should ignore the biblical teachings on justice and morality? What of modern laws and regulations?

References: Helen MacInnes, *While Still We Live*. New York: Fawcett Crest, 1944, p. 81. (1) Romans 1:19-23. (2) Luke 11:35-36; 1 John 1:5-10. (3) John 15:12-17. (4) Leviticus 19:13-14. (5) Matthew 5:17-20. (6) Matthew 23:3-4. (7) Matthew 23:23, 25. (8) Adapted from Luke 10:25-37. (9) James 2:14-17. (10) Matthew 7:1-5; Romans 14:4.

6. Even Though I Walk Through the Darkest Valley . . . What does the story of Job say about surviving the bad times in life? Do your friends understand what has happened in your life? What have your own dark valleys told you about yourself? What are you willing to live for?

References: Luke Timothy Johnson, "Learning Jesus," *The Christian Century*, 12/2/98. (1) Matthew 4:1-11; Job 1:9-12. (2) Job 1:21. (3) Job 2:3, NAB. (4) Job 2:4-5. (5) Job 2:9. (6) Job 2:11-13. (7) Job 4:1-8. (8) Job 4:17-19. (9) Job 5:8-14. (10) Job 5:17-27. (11) Job 6:8-10. (12) Job 6:28-30 paraphrased. (13) Job 7:19-21, paraphrased. (14) Job 8:4-7, 20. (15) Job 9:15-24. (16) Job 9:32-35. (17) Job 10:2. (18) Job 11:4. (19) Job 12:5, 7-14. (20) Job 16:2; 19:2-3. (21) Job 15:5-6; 18:5-8; 22:4-5; 21-27. (22) Job 16:19; 19:23-27. (23) Job 23:2-4. (24) Job 21:7-15. (25) Job 38—41.

7. I Fear No Evil; for You Are with Me . . . What are the fears your friends and co-workers share with you? Is it better to acknowledge our fears or deny them? Recall the life events that have made an impact on you. What might God have been trying to shape in your character? Which experience of faith has shown you God's ability to ease your fears and anxieties? How has the experience of others given you confidence in God?

References: Thomas Merton, "Prayer of Trust and Confidence," Catholic Campus Ministries, James Madison University. (1) Luke 12:4-7; Matthew 10:28-31. (2) John 14:15-17. (3) Ephesians 3:16-21. (4) Romans 8:31-39, note vv. 38-39. (5) Romans 8:14. (6) 1 Corinthians 10:13. (7) Matthew 26:36-39. (8) Mark 15:34. (9) Matthew 13:1-9. (10) Matthew 15:21-28. (11) Mark 16:1-8; Luke 24:1-12; Matthew 28:1-7. (12) John 20:11-18. (13) John 20:19-21;

Luke 24:36-43. (14) John 20:24-29, paraphrased. (15) Luke 24:13-35. (16) Acts 9:1-9; 22:1-15.

8. Your Rod and Your Staff—They Comfort Me . . . How would you define discipline? How much of it is physical? mental? spiritual? At what point in life should discipline begin? Which discipline do you find easiest to ignore? At what point is discipline no longer required? What do we risk in refusing the discipline of God?

References: Proverbs 3:11-12. (1) Matthew 23:23-26. (2) The lifelong nature of discipleship is implied in many of the sayings and parables of Jesus, for example, Matthew 7:14, the narrow gate and hard road to life, also the vine branches that are pruned to bear fruit, John 15:1-8. (3) For human "feelings" versus godlike actions, see Luke 6:27-35. (4) John 3:1-21. (5) Ephesians 4:14-15; 22-24; 2 Corinthians 5:17. (6) See Acts 22 for a brief note on Paul's background. (7) Acts 9:2; 11:26. (8) Acts 6:1-6. (9) Acts 8:26-38. (10) Acts 7. (11) Acts 26:9-10. (12) Acts 26:15-18. (13) 1 Corinthians 15:9. (14) Acts 22:10. (15) Mark 1:15. (16) Ephesians 4:17-32.

9. You Prepare a Table Before Me in the Presence of My Enemies . . . Why is overcoming sin a part of becoming like the image of God? But if God wants us that way, why are some sins so hard to overcome? What are the enemies you may have created in yourself? Which ones echo or respond to what is less than good in others? How have time pressures contributed to problems created by your inner enemies? What are the evidences of the power God uses to overcome your enemies?

References: (1) Acts 14:19. (2) Acts 16:22-24. (3) Acts 21:30-31. (4) Ephesians 6:12. (5) Ezekiel 12:2; John 9:39-41. (6) Romans 5:8. (7) John 1:12-13. (8) Matthew 5:2-12; 7:7-11.

10. You Anoint My Head with Oil; My Cup Overflows

. . . What privileges are extended to those who eat of the Lord's table? Compare the symbolism of the seder meal and communion. What features express the breakthrough of God's kingdom reality? How? In what way is marriage supposed to be a picture of the *What Is* of God?

References: Thomas J. Porter, Gather Comprehensive, Chicago: GIA Publications, 1994, No. 816. (1) Mark 1:11, NAB. (2) Genesis 3:1-7. (3) Daniel 1:3-17. (4) Exodus 12. (5) Exodus 12:47. (6) Exodus 12:11, 39. (7) Exodus 12:13. (8) Matthew 26:26-28. (9) John 13:3-17. (10) Ephesians 5:25-33.

11. Surely Goodness and Mercy Shall Follow Me All the Days of My Life

. . . Where have you seen goodness, mercy, and integrity in business situations? In community conditions? How can God use the stress in your life to help you to grow in his integrity? As you made choices of integrity, how have you experienced the goodness and mercy of God?

References: John W. Whitehead, Cryptoquote, (c) 1989, King Features Syndicate, Inc. (1) T. H. Holmes and R. H. Rahe, "The Social Readjustment Rating Scale," *Journal of Psychosomatic Research,* 11 (1967) pp. 213-218, cited in Selye, *Stress in Health and Disease,* p. 677. (2) Romans 5:1-5. (3) 1 Corinthians 10:13. (4) John 14:2. (5) Published in 1998 by Herald Press. (6) Psalm 37:5. (7) Matthew 18:19-20. (8) Proverbs 3:5-

6. (9) Romans 8:28. (10) Hans Selye, M.D., *Stress Without Distress*, New York: Signet, 1975, p. 140. (11) Isaiah 40:31. (12) Philippians 2:12-13. (13) Galatians 1:6-12; 1 Timothy 1:3-7. (14) Ephesians 6:10-17, for this and the three following paragraphs. (15) Hebrews 4:12. (16) Ephesians 6:18.

12. And I Shall Dwell in the House of the Lord My Whole Life Long . . . What advantages are there for you in working with others of faith? How may they help you work out your place in God's reality? Some persons give up on their weaknesses. In what ways can the people of God help? How can being disciples together reinforce the disciplines of God? What does forgiveness mean to you? Have you found and accepted your place in the body of Christ? How might your life change as you go on in faith? In what way have your ideas of stress changed?

References: Larry Letich, "Is Life Outsmarting Us?" *The Washington Post*, April 2, 1995. (1) John 10:16. (2) 1 Corinthians 12. (3) Ephesians 2:11-22. (4) John 15:4-9; 14:12-14. (5) John 6:56-57. (6) John 6:60, NAB. (7) Hebrews 12:1-2. (8) Matthew 26:69-75. (9) Acts 11:26. (10) Galatians 2:11-14 (Cephas is Aramaic for Peter). (11) Isaiah 55:6, 7; Micah 7:18. (12) Luke 6:36-38; 7:36-50; 11:4. (13) Luke 11:9-13; 17:20-21. (14) Philippians 4:8-9. (15) Philippians 2:3-15. (16) 1 Corinthians 15:42-58.

The Author

James Fairfield began his study of stress, supported in part by a grant from Mennonite Mutual Aid, in 1977, when he faced radical surgery for cancer, a disease some experts identify with undue stress. Stress remained a topic of interest as he completed his Master of Arts in Religion in 1982 from Eastern Mennonite University.

As a communicator Jim has worked for Mennonite Media Ministries, wrote for Leighton Ford's daily television show, edited books, and started Creative Counselors. His writings have appeared in a number of magazines and newspapers in Canada and the United States. This is his fifth book published by Herald Press.

Jim and his wife, Norma, live on a small farm in the Shenandoah Valley of Virginia. They have four children and twelve grandchildren.